P9-DGT-100

The Hedge

TWENTIETH-CENTURY CONTINENTAL FICTION

THE HEDGE

MIGUEL DELIBES

Translated from the Spanish by
Frances M. López-Morillas

New York COLUMBIA UNIVERSITY PRESS *1983*

The Press wishes to acknowledge the assistance of the
Comité Conjunto Hispano-Norteamericano para
Asuntos Educativos y Culturales
in the preparation of this translation.

Library of Congress Cataloging in Publication Data
Delibes, Miguel.
The hedge.
(Twentieth-Century Continental Fiction)
Translation of: Parábola del náufrago.
I. Title. II. Series.
PQ6607.E45P2513 1983   863'.64   83-7567
ISBN 0-231-05460-2

Spanish original: *Parábola del náufrago*
© 1969 Ediciones Destino

Columbia University Press
New York   Guildford, Surrey

*Clothbound editions of Columbia University Press books are
Smyth-sewn and printed on permanent and durable acid-free paper.*

For Jacinto San José
For Giacint Sviatoi Iosif

My principal emotion is fear.
—MAX HORKHEIMER

FIRST came the street with the zebra-striped pedestrian crossing, then the sidewalk of gray hexagonal paving blocks, then the fence with iron bars finished off in arrowhead shapes, then the garden (dwarfed little garden plots of box, floral borders, and climbing roses, with cinder paths zigzagging through the carefully tended green grass) and, finally, on the green hill, the massive white marble building with wide rectangular windows overlooking the garden and, up above, presiding over it all, the winking illuminated sign: DON ABDON, LTD.

equals equals =
period = .
comma = ,
semicolon = ;
colon = :
quotation marks = " "
parenthesis = (
close parenthesis =)
exclamation point = !
question mark = ?

Behind the fence comma to the right of the gate comma beside the larch tree comma was the little house of Genaro parenthesis now called Gen colon Here, Gen; come Gen! close parenthesis comma like a dollhouse comma white too comma with a gray slate roof and when it rained or Baudelio Villamayor the gardener parenthesis in whose greenhouse Jacinto started his movement Through Silence to Peace close parenthesis used the hose comma the gray slate roof turned black and shiny as if newly varnished period And every morning when he came to work comma Jacinto would hear Gen stirring even before he got inside the fence comma his chain scraping on the floorboards of the doghouse comma his warm noisy yawn and finally comma from the corner comma he would see Gen's head appear in the doorhole comma his long floppy ears lying limply on his cheeks comma his brow wrinkled and furrowed comma the pained humility of his hazel eyes fixed upon him and comma around his neck comma the heavy leash with the steel ring where the clip of his chain was fastened period Gen's busy behind comma which was gradually growing fuzz comma moved delightedly from side to side while Jacinto drummed rap-rap-ratatat with two fingers on the slate top and murmured hello there Gen, how are you, and then Gen would stretch setting his hands firmly on the ground and stretching his arms as much as he could and then comma before he jumped up on Jacinto's chest comma he would take the precaution of standing close to the trunk of the larch tree comma raising one leg and peeing period When he had finished comma Gen would open his legs comma scratch with his hands until he had covered the little wet patch with cinders and jump up on him comma fawning on him and staining the lapels of his gray suit with dirt comma while Jacinto said hello there Gen, quiet Gen, that's enough Gen don't you think? but Gen did not answer rather with his capering he seemed to be carrying out a preliminary attempt to reach the tip of Jacinto's nose with his tongue and Jacinto would scold him that's enough Gen; lie down! until Gen restrained himself comma stretched his arms out in front of him comma buried his head in them comma closed his eyes comma wrinkled his brow comma tensed his limbs and let out a yawn so prodigious that you would have said he was about to dislocate his jaws period After his great yawn Genaro would calm down and let Jacinto scratch him between the eyes for a few minutes comma in the shallow furrow that had formed between his eyes comma just above his nose comma half closing his eyelids comma quiet now comma as if in a trance comma and then Jacinto would talk to him in honeyed tones Gen, you old wheedler, you know I don't forget you comma but comma as soon as Jacinto stopped scratching him comma Gen would start to jump up on him again and Jacinto would have to scold him that's enough Gen, down! and Gen would wriggle his behind again comma lower his head and wag it violently from side to side and his long floppy ears would strike against his cheeks with a noise like faraway applause or clothes slapping on a wind-whipped clothesline period Then comma as Jacinto fed him one by one some dried chestnuts or cookies or meat scraps comma Genaro would snap up the offering without tasting it comma without chewing it even comma

3

with such avidity that often his upper teeth would clash against the lower ones chomp after he had swallowed the mouthful comma despite Jacinto's warnings comma eat slowly Gen, nobody's going to take it away from you, it can't do you any good that way comma but Gen was already peering at his hand and comma sometimes comma too impatient to wait comma would leap at it comma at his hand comma until Jacinto would open the pincers of his fingers and let go of the cookie or the dried chestnut or the scrap of meat and Gen's long outsized mouth would catch it greedily in the air end of paragraph

Genaro had changed a great deal and yet that transformation didn't seem to affect him semicolon you might say that he accepted the new situation willingly and even if Darío Esteban aimed a kick at him comma he never protested comma quite the opposite comma he accepted the punishment as well deserved comma humbly bent his elbows and knees and with his belly hugging the ground he would take refuge in the doghouse and comma once inside comma he would curl up and gaze at his attacker from just inside the doorhole with bloodshot comma imploring eyes end of paragraph

At first comma Genaro slept stretched out at full length comma but comma by a few weeks after his demotion comma he gradually began to bend at the waist and two months later he would curl up like a snail period Jacinto liked that way better because it meant that his privates were hidden and between this and the thick soft spotted fuzz that was gradually spreading over his back parenthesis even over and between the little protuberances formed by his vertebrae close parenthesis his nudity

4

seemed more bearable comma although this too didn't seem to bother Genaro unduly comma indeed during the first few days comma Jacinto could have sworn that Gen was taking satisfaction in displaying his body because every time he felt the urge comma he would stretch out voluptuously in the sun at full length or lie on his side in the dappled shade of the larch tree when the sun became too hot comma unself-consciously comma shamelessly showing his private parts and comma as sometimes happened comma he didn't hesitate to fall asleep that way period Genaro had submitted to his new duties without making a fuss and comma conscious that prudence was the most important thing demanded of him comma maintained silence comma an ominous silence which Darío Esteban often broke by aiming a kick at him for no other reason than his silence period At first comma at appropriate intervals comma Genaro would ask for bread and water but later he became more subdued and could go on and on without eating or drinking or comma at most comma during the dog days he would ask for water in a cracked voice and comma at last comma convinced that it made no difference comma he eventually just said wa comma probably so as not to wear himself out comma but as he insisted and kept raising his voice wa-wa-wa! comma his plea comma especially when heard at a distance comma produced the effect of barking period The rest of the time Gen didn't say anything comma he kept still comma and was obviously contented and grateful comma an attitude that showed up as much in the unctuous fawnings with which he received his fellow employees daily comma as in the disproportionate joy with which he welcomed comma after saying wa-wa-wa! a couple of dozen times comma the rusty can that Jacinto brought him filled with water from the fountain in the garden period At such times comma Jacinto was amazed by Genaro's skill comma by his new and surprising way of drinking comma without lifting the can from the ground or touching it with his hand comma but comma simply comma lowering his head and lapping the surface of the water with his tongue parenthesis which along with his ears and canine teeth had developed a lot close parenthesis eagerly and delicately at one and the same time comma so that he was able to empty it without spilling a single drop period Sometimes comma on sultry days comma Gen comma after having his drink comma would keep on looking at him earnestly comma his mouth hanging open comma his long pink tongue dangling comma panting comma and then Jacinto would go back to the fountain comma fill the can again and set it on the ground comma within Gen's reach period Already a silent language had come into existence between Jacinto and Genaro which made words unnecessary end of paragraph

Later, in the washroom (gentlemen), Jacinto would scrub his hands with soap powder and talk to himself in the mirror as he had the habit of doing, *so Genaro is happier than before, I'm telling you, Jacinto, ever so much happier, don't tell me, he was always complaining about his wife, or about his kids, every day harping on something, a real whiner . . . And now, there he is, you take him a bone and fine, perfectly happy, and you don't take him one and fine too, because don't think he misses it, or worries, or gets cross,*

*or anything at all. And the fact is, d'you know what's the
bad thing about our situation, Jacinto, huh? Well, it's this:
stop and think, because I still remember the day Genaro threw
up that stew because he spotted a fly in the sauce just as he
was finishing it, how about that? Gosh, look at him now.
And the fly isn't the bad part, Jacinto, you can be sure of
that, but thinking about the fly, that's right, because if you
don't think about the fly it's as if the fly didn't exist. Catch
on? What happens is that we get more squeamish every day
and that's what makes us the way we are. That's why I'm
tipping you off that if what Don Abdón wants is to keep us
from thinking about the fly, then more power to Don Abdón,
Don Abdón is an honorable man because he wants us not to
think about the fly for the simple reason that he knows that
thinking about the fly means putting up with the fly, and if
that's not so, there's Genaro, it's as clear as crystal, you see
him now, right? well, just think what he used to be like,
what a pain in the neck, Jacinto, gosh, for heaven's sake,
always complaining about his wife, or his kids, or his salary,
a really boring guy, don't tell me. But now it's a pleasure to
see him, really, Jacinto, why make things more complicated
than they are, his wife grabs hold of the leash and off they
go for a walk, a run, he's more relaxed than anybody else,
sniffing the hollows in the tree trunks, lifting his leg on corners, wherever he feels the urge, just look at him, he almost
always does it out of childishness, don't you believe it, about
ninety percent of the time, and even then I'm underestimat-
ing, practically nothing, a few drops, it's just like I'm telling
you, why, he doesn't bother anybody, that's what I say, and
he likes it, he's doing just fine . . . But it's different with
her, whoo! I don't need to tell you, Jacinto, you can see a*

7

mile off that she's having a bad time, and d'you know why? Well, for the simple reason that she's thinking about the fly, that's the only reason, it's anybody's guess, she surely must be ashamed of leading her husband like that, or having her women friends see him on all fours, or naked, it's her friends, that kind of thing, prejudices, after all, who knows whether one thing is just the same as another, huh? and if Genaro likes to wander around out there as naked as the day he was born, jumping up and down or snuggling up to street corners, you tell me Jacinto if it's important whether you have four feet or two, it's all the same in the end, and if he's happy like that, well leave him alone, for gosh sakes, if everything were no worse than that, because after all, if thinking is what makes us suffer, then why the dickens do we think at all?

Jacinto standing there, at first sight, turns out to be a very ordinary man: neither tall nor short, neither fat nor thin, neither particularly neat nor a careless dresser; a run-of-the-mill man with blue eyes (pale gray when near the sea, which Jacinto yearns for, or on misty afternoons), hazy and watery as the sun that begins to break through the fog on winter days. Jacinto gives the impression of being nearsighted and perhaps he is. But it isn't easy to ascertain whether he is nearsighted or not nearsighted, for in the office, though he works near the big window (from which he can see Gen's doghouse), he holds papers very close to his nose and, on the other hand, nobody, and I mean nobody, has ever seen him use glasses, not even at the movies, even though they are showing films in the original language with subtitles.

8

Jacinto's calligraphy is extremely careful, English style as well as roundhand as well as, in exceptional cases (for example, when he is doing a special-assignment parchment), Gothic and Carolingian, whose letters he draws with impeccable precision and neatness. As he writes he squints a little out of his left eye while with the hand on that same side he tirelessly turns round and round the gold medal which, ever since he can remember (and hence even longer than that), has hung from his neck. None of this diminishes the firmness of his strokes (the strokes of his calligraphy), which he performs unhesitatingly, all in one movement, so that there is no break between the light strokes and the heavy ones, that is, one slips into the heavy lines of the letters fluidly, unconsciously, as into the eddy of a river near a rapids or a gully. In his work he uses three colors of ink: blue, green, and red, blue for epigraphs (when they exist, which they rarely do), and red and green for numerals, and three types of calligrapher's nibs: crown nib, gooseneck nib, Renaissance nib, which he changes, every time he needs to, without loss of time but also without haste, and which he moistens slightly with the tip of his tongue (the first time he uses them) to make the ink stay on.

He (Jacinto) appears to be a rather meticulous man and he yearns for personal security. A few months ago he went through a very uneasy period when he observed the progress made by the adding machines in the office, thinking that expert calligraphers were a dying breed, but Don Abdón, who is a father to everyone, reassured him with his end-of-the-year speech, when he said that the most perfect electronic brain wasn't worthy to untie the shoes of a good solid craftsman. That was what Don Abdón said, Don Abdón who is a father to everyone, and this calmed Jacinto, who often, in view of the conquests of technology, believes that he is dispensable and lives off charity.

Jacinto's pallor is surprising; his is a translucent pallor, like that of fine porcelain, scarcely shadowed, on his face, by the extremely slight trace of his beard, which is very blond, as is his hair. Jacinto's pallor has a certain property: it accentuates the colors of the objects he (Jacinto) approaches, it darkens the most spotless paper, and black, near him, takes on the funereal quality of jet. Because of the white transparency of his skin, Jacinto's veins cast blue shadows on some parts of his body, especially his temples and wrists, which leads Amando García, his officemate, to tell him that his wrists and temples match his eyes.

Jacinto is neither obstinate nor indifferent. He shows respect to his superiors, perhaps out of an innate feeling of submissiveness, perhaps because the historico-social context (as César Fuentes says in his piping eunuch's voice) does not lend itself to anything else, perhaps because rebelliousness (thinks Jacinto) is a source of discord, perhaps, in a word, because he (Jacinto) is timid, and the mere presence (of his boss) frightens him. In any case he is a respectable and responsible employee, and when Darío Esteban, the monitor, elbows resting on the railing of his logwood minaret, in the center of the big circular room, focuses his binoculars on his subordinates, he rarely pauses on him (Jacinto) because he (Darío Esteban) undoubtedly knows that Jacinto is a scrupulous employee who has never been obstructive or disputed the postulate "order is freedom" which rules the establishment. Don Abdón does not express these postulates lightly; rather, he thinks them through, and last Christmas he supported his dictum by an indisputable dialectic process, structured into five causally linked phases (order-labor, labor-efficiency, efficiency-productivity, productivity-purchasing power, and purchasing power-freedom), concluding bathetically with tears in his eyes, "My children, can you imagine a free man without a coin in his pocket?"

That's what Don Abdón said last Christmas and all of them, beginning with Amando García, agreed and applauded loudly German-style, that is, repeatedly banging the tops of their desks on the drawers beneath until the ink slopped out of the inkwells.

Since Jacinto is anxious to do his job well, he does not mind the logwood minaret, nor the binoculars, nor the fact that he is monitored, things which, for instance, annoy his officemate Ginés Gil (though he hides the fact). Naturally Jacinto does not object either to standing up in a disciplined way, in unison with his officemates, when Don Abdón arrives, or to synchronizing his voice with the other voices, obeying the baton of Darío Esteban from his minaret: AD-DING-IS-THE-NO-BLEST-AC-TI-VI-TY-OF-MAN-ON-THIS-PLAN-ET, or: TALK-ING-A-BOUT-SPORTS-IS-EVEN-HEALTH-IER-THAN-PRAC-TI-CING-THEM, or: A-VOI-DING-RE-SPON-SI-BIL-I-TY-IS-THE-

11

FIRST-STEP-TO-WARD-BE-ING-HAPPY, either one or another, for the slogans vary according to the season and the circumstances.

Suddenly the voice of Darío Esteban, the monitor, would thunder over the loudspeakers:

"Sit down, hup!"

To say "Sit down, hup!" Darío Esteban brings his baritone voice up from the depths of his chest, just as, when he wants to scold the clerks persuasively on occasion, he uses his bass voice. Darío Esteban has at his disposal an infinite variety of vocal registers. Darío Esteban's face is broad and plump but inscrutable, and his movements and manners are cautious (with the cautiousness characteristic of a versatile man) and deliberate (with the deliberateness of a cautious man). His hands, though stubby, are large and well cared for, and the ring that clasps the middle finger of his right hand inspires an almost pastoral respect among his subordinates.

And so Darío Esteban would command, "Sit down, hup!" in his baritone voice, and in view of his order, everyone sat down and resumed his interrupted task and, from that moment onward and throughout the working day, no other sound was heard in the big room but the metallic tickrattleclick of the adding machines and the scratching, scree-scree, of the expert calligraphers' pens on paper. Darío Esteban, meanwhile, peered around him with the binoculars, leaning his elbows on the railing of the minaret like a sailor on the bridge, and, from time to time, he would address one of the desks by dictaphone to chide its occupant paternally or punish him by making him kneel facing the wall or write "I must work hard," a thousand times at recess. Also, once in a blue moon (two or three times a year) Darío Esteban would interrupt the collective task by banging on a gong, boinnng!, and, when the last vibration had died away, would explain, "Daniel Gómez, one billion. Let us congratulate ourselves on the sum achieved by this fellowworker."

Two hundred faces with the bluish pallor of paper would look up from the paper simultaneously and a ripple of admiration, like a rising sea, would emerge from the army of clerks, while Darío Esteban, with his broad watermelon smile, solemnly descended from his minaret and, tiptoeing over the soft thick carpet, headed for the mahogany door at the back of the room, gave a tug to his navy-blue suit jacket, adjusted his tie, pressed the button of the bell protected by a gold plate, waited a few seconds for the pilot light to turn green, gave a little cough of collusion, and, at last, went into that office to which no one but himself had access.

But now Jacinto is there, and this makes him tremble like a leaf and feel a weakness in his joints (chiefly his knees) and a crampy sensation in the pit of his stomach, until he is seated on the three-legged stool, and Don Abdón breaks the silence, and the first thing Don Abdón says to him is, "You're timid, aren't you?"

There are perhaps other more important things to talk about, like salaries, discipline, or the organization of the Company, undoubtedly there are (subjects to talk about), but this is the first thing Don Abdón says to him, making his voice sound solemn and repeatedly pinching the tips of his nipples, "You're timid, aren't you?" And Ja-

13

cinto, seated on the stool, looks at him (Don Abdón) up there, framed by the golden baldachin, inaccessible, above the base of Carrara marble, a chorus of blond, winged children decorating the lofty cupola. But in order to see him (Don Abdón), Jacinto must tip his head violently backward and stretch his neck as far as it (the neck) will go, to the point that his Adam's apple is squeezed and he feels a sharp pain (owing to the weight of his head) in the bulge of the first cervical vertebra. And when Don Abdón asks him if he is timid, he (Jacinto) assents, half fainting on the stool, he simply nods his head twice, as much to assent as to relieve the double tension temporarily.

Jacinto feels confused in that immense empty room, full of resounding concavities (canopy, niches, cupola), paved with white marble, with the steps and base and the golden baldachin (which has twisted Solomonic columns) and the trumpeter cherubs up above, and the scribes, copyists, and printers on the lateral frescoes, each of them (scribes, copyists, and printers) of a particular period and all of them (scribes, copyists, and printers) relentlessly carrying out cabalistic arithmetical operations. And to top off the extraordinary picture, Don Abdón, squatting above the altar, his arms crossed over the naked maternal teats, black-nippled, like a Buddha. Don Abdón's swollen breasts produce a complex sensation in Jacinto, a mixture of attraction, confusion, and rapture. In the swimming pool, Don Abdón usually covers them (his breasts) with a red polka-dotted brassiere, but now he shows them naked, turgid and pointed as two melons. And he (Jacinto) is obsessed by the blackness of the nipples and confusedly senses that Darío Esteban is right when he proclaims, "Don Abdón is the most motherly father of all fathers." And there, in Don Abdón's sheltering and welcoming pectoral swellings, he (Jacinto) guesses that his lost security lies concealed. But how to attain it? He (Jacinto) cannot think. He feels identified with those blond, blue-eyed children who decorate the cupola and hold aloft, as if carelessly (without interrupting their games), a red-lettered gilded sign which forms curlicues at both ends and reads: ORDER IS FREEDOM. But Jacinto is startled because, along with the breasts, are Don Abdón's tight knotty biceps, in paradoxical contrast to his black nourishing nipples, and those muscles next to the jiggling swellings make him (Jacinto) uneasy, as if he were to surprise a man and a woman naked, clinging to each other. "Motherly lap and strong arm," is what Darío Esteban is wont to say to express desirable authority symbolically: "Don Abdón is the most motherly father of all fathers." That's right. And there he looms, commanding and silent, squatting, framed by the canopy and the golden baldachin, under the chubby-cheeked children blowing trumpets. And the first thing he (Don Abdón) says to Jacinto is, "You're timid, aren't you?"

And Jacinto assents, bobs his head twice, wordlessly, because his voice has choked in his throat and also because the pressure on his Adam's apple and the pain in the back of his neck are becoming unbearable. And so he (Jacinto) assents, seated on the edge of the stool, and then Don Abdón makes his hybrid voice sound hollow and says, "For the timid man, the solution is a hedge."

"A hedge?" his (Jacinto's) voice comes out like a moan, cracked and rasping, and he (Jacinto) smiles in a puzzled way, because Doña Palmira usually says to him when she catches him watering the begonia, the sansevieria, or the ficus, she usually says, "That's a job for young ladies, Master Jacinto." Hence Jacinto smiles when he asks Don Abdón, "A hedge?"

But all this happened several days after Jacinto got dizzy in the office when he wrote zeroes.

Each quarter and at the end of the year, Don Abdón would personally award the Prizes for Adders, consisting of a Diploma and a sum of money, and it was not infrequent that, at the close of the ceremony, he would break down and, with tears in his eyes, tell them that the Company was theirs and that, in consequence, by bringing honor to the Company they brought honor on themselves. Indeed, Don Abdón had revolutionized the place and all its activities and every comment now turned on him, and people said, "We were nothing till he came; we owe everything to his initiative," and Doña Palmira herself often acknowledged in Jacinto's presence, "Thanks to Don Abdón we are what we are." The mere fact of speaking Don Abdón's name on the street was reason enough for men to take off their hats and women to murmur reverently, "He's a father and a mother to everyone," and even, when Genaro was demoted, people commented, "Anyone else would have beaten him up and kicked him out of the city," that was what they said, and so, when he (Don Abdón) paraded through the streets in his cherry-colored car, he aroused spontaneous ovations and displays of affection and the young moth-

16

ers, insistently, held their babies up to the windows of the cherry-colored car so that Don Abdón could fondle their blond heads.

On some winter afternoons, Don Abdón would go to the movies or the theater, and in those cases, the girls in the box office would not sell the seat in front of him, so that no one would interfere with his visibility, and the adjoining seats, so that Don Abdón could recline first on one side and then on the other without anyone's being in his way. A still greater commotion was produced in summer by his arrival at the swimming pool, hymned by loudspeakers with the march "He's the Only One," to whose strains people climbed out of the water and clustered on the edges of the pool waiting for him (Don Abdón) to appear in his white bikini with the red polka dots and the green life ring circling his waist. Don Abdón was not tall, but his burgeoning and massive appearance inspired confidence in his fellow citizens, who were wont to say, "We have a man who will last a while." From his hips to his neck, Don Abdón's figure narrowed like a conic section, and his solid, powerful neck, sprinkled with freckles (if he sunbathed the girls would cover each individual freckle with confetti, realizing that one of those splotches, in the course of time, might degenerate into something malignant), was topped off by a flat skull of an Aryan type, with the grizzled hair in a crew cut. And when Don Abdón, holding on to the white ladder, sprinkled water on the nape of his neck and his stomach, all present smiled and nudged each other and said, "He's trying to guard against congestion; he's no fool, no indeed." And when, at last, he plunged in, a

17

devout silence ensued all around, and, after some preliminary and futile arm movements, he waited for the
cry, "Without the life ring, Don Abdón!" and he (Don
Abdón), to humor them, would slip the life ring over his
head, swell out the back of his neck and splash about,
thrashing his arms and legs without coordinating his
movements, so that those of his feet neutralized those of
his arms, leaving him motionless, like a kestrel hanging
in the air. The bathers would agree, "Just look at the
progress he's made! It hardly seems possible in so few
years," and then someone a little bolder than the others
would say, "Under water for a bit, Don Abdón!" and he,
Don Abdón, needing no further encouragement, would
stick his square head under the water for a few seconds
and kick away madly at the water, but he never succeeded in making his broad spotted behind disappear
beneath the surface. Notwithstanding, the bathers' admiration took the form of demands: "Don Abdón, a bellywhop!" "Don Abdón, breast stroke!" "Now in the deep
end, Don Abdón!" and Don Abdón graciously acceded
to the requests, and "How considerate he is!" remarked
the bathers, and, once the audience was satisfied, Don
Abdón would emerge and, as he wrapped himself in the
red bathrobe that Honesto held out to him, people would
applaud him affectionately until he disappeared into the
blue and white striped tent (ten times more spacious than
Gen's quarters).

Don Abdón inspired waves of affection everywhere he
went and, if some outsider happened to come to the city,
people hastened to tell him, "Before he arrived, this was
all dead, good and dead, and now look." And if by

chance a famous orchestra was performing in the city and Don Abdón unexpectedly appeared at the concert, the audience, filled with enthusiasm, would demand that the conductor let him take over some instrument, perhaps the flute, perhaps the clavichord, perhaps the trombone, and at the end, inevitably, the performance would be topped off with a solo by Don Abdón on the bass drum. Applause thundered out, and everyone in the audience would exchange looks and signs of approval and remark, "What skill! Anyone would say that he'd spent his life doing nothing else."

Jacinto feels toward Don Abdón a reverent (or in any case cautious) admiration or fear. Instinctively he seems to be grateful that even though Don Abdón has power he does not use it against him. In past months, before the invasion of the adding machines, Jacinto feared that he would lose his job, but Don Abdon's end-of-the-year speech left him feeling more relaxed. Don Abdón said on that occasion, to everyone who cared to listen, that the best electronic brain wasn't fit to untie the shoes of a good solid craftsman, that is what Don Abdón said at the time of the end-of-the-year celebrations, and since Jacinto is aware that he is a more than solid expert calligrapher, he was left feeling quite calm. Perhaps, at bottom, Jacinto feels intuitively that Don Abdón is watching over him and when Amando García or Ginés Gil, another fellow just like him, talk after work or in the Refectory about Old Palindrome or Horny Otis he (Jacinto) pretends not to notice and acts as if he does not hear them, for though on the one hand he is respectful of his superiors (or seems to be), on the other hand he does not like to become (or fears to become) an informer. That is why he pretends he isn't listening, although for the malicious gossips, and there are always some of those, Don Abdón is called Old Palindrome or Horny Otis. The name Old Palindrome, though it isn't a perfect one, is easy to see (Don Ab-don) and the nickname of Horny Otis, though it's more farfetched, has a basis in fact, as explained by Ginés Gil, an expert hunter, according to which the Great Bustard (whose Latin name is Otis), when it comes into heat in the spring, swells its neck monstrously, and, in view of the fact that Don Abdón's neck is an apoplectic, robust, and reddish feature which is all of a piece with the back of his head, the name of Horny Otis makes a certain amount of sense when applied to him. However, Jacinto, who is naturally honest and respectful to his superiors, never uses nicknames, neither with those higher than he nor with those lower in the scale, and calls everyone by his Christian name. He only calls Genaro Martín "Gen" out of force of habit since his demotion, perhaps because the fact that he now goes on all fours and raises his hind legs on street corners and in the hollows of trees seems to make the monosyllable necessary, but in any case the monosyllable is not a contemptuous one because he values Gen greatly and interceded for him (for Gen) when it was necessary and every time he sees him he scratches him between the eyes or gives him an affectionate pat on the ribs.

Besides being honest, Jacinto is peaceable and kindly, or perhaps he (Jacinto) is cowardly, but he prefers to pass for a nonviolent person rather than for a coward; the fact is that he avoids confrontations, though on the other hand he (Jacinto) is not given to half-truths, and if a request seems fair to him he does not hesitate to express it or support it. Generally speaking he (Jacinto) tries to protect the weak, though it must be said that he does not put too much enthusiasm into the task, maybe out of fear that the anger, insolence, or cruelty of stronger men may turn against him. This is the case, for example, of the hazings organized by Amando García or the jokes he (Amando García also) plays on the street when he pretends to be drunk or lame or blind and makes cars brake angrily or asks pretty girls to help him cross the street and, once across, bugs out his eyes, wiggles his ears in a very peculiar way, plants a kiss on their (the girls') cheeks and says, "Thanks, honey, I never saw such beautiful eyes in my life." César Fuentes says of him (of Amando García) that he has a gelded heart, like all weaklings. César Fuentes' wound still festers and for him everybody is gelded in one place or another, though Ginés Gil explains that the trouble with César Fuentes is that he's a sorehead who doesn't know how to take a joke.

César Fuentes has stuck close to Jacinto ever since he entered the Company, perhaps because the day he arrived Jacinto was the only one who interceded for him and tried to dissuade his officemates from their intentions, pointing out to them that he (César Fuentes) had just arrived from a small town, but Amando García said, "A country boy, that's the frosting on the cake," and he made him go up on the rooftop terrace with everyone trooping up after them and he tied a cord to his scrotum and a brick to the other end (running the cord through the hole in the center of the brick) and everybody laughed and Amando García said to César Fuentes, comically wiggling his ears, "Now throw the brick over the railing, go on," and César Fuentes answered him (Amando García), "Gosh, no, I could get hurt," and Jacinto gave César Fuentes a conspiratorial wink, tipping him off that Ginés Gil would cut the cord in time and worse wouldn't come to worst, that is, that it was a joke, but Ginés Gil, either because there was a nick in the knifeblade (as he said afterward, adopting a slyly regretful attitude and scrutinizing the blade) or maybe because he wanted to stretch out the hazing to the last instant, failed this time, for whatever reason he didn't cut the cord and, after much hesitation (on the part of César Fuentes), the brick went sailing violently over the retaining wall taking with it the testicles of César Fuentes who, when he felt the tearing sensation and observed that everyone around him was howling with laughter, turned ashen and fainted and Amando García, amid the general hilarity, looked over the parapet and said, "Well, what the fuck, if old Gen hasn't eaten the country boy's things!" and, in view of this unexpected development, the gales of laughter grew louder, but as César Fuentes gave no signs of coming to, despite the fact that Jacinto trotted back and forth to the restroom and put cotton pads soaked in water on his forehead, the officemates decided that the joke was over and came down from the roof, in groups of three or four, talking about the events of the hazing (César Fuentes' face before and after, Gen's gluttony, Amando García's cleverness) and the poor showing the new man had made, while Jacinto came and went from the toilet (gentlemen) and put Mercurochrome on the torn-off scrotum. When he came to, César Fuentes' first words were, "Did that bunch of fairies get my balls?" he said, and Jacinto said yes, and when he surprised a rebellious expression on César Fuentes' face, he tried to soothe him:

"Don't worry about it," he said, "nowadays they can work wonders with all that stuff about transplants."

César Fuentes kept yelling, his hands held between his legs, and with each yell he bled some more, and in view of this Jacinto notified Darío Esteban who, when he took in the situation, couldn't help laughing and scolded César Fuentes and said, in his solemn bass voice, if they didn't ever play jokes in his home town, that it was a sign of discourtesy to lose one's temper over a joke, that hazing was what made a man tough, and lastly, that he shouldn't worry about such a trifling thing, that masculine attributes were no use for adding figures and that the Company had enough Rest and Recuperation Homes to accommodate all its employees at once and that that was precisely the glory of the Company, but, when César Fuentes returned from the Rest and Recuperation Home, Jacinto could see that the hazing, far from making him tough, had weakened him: along with the strength of his muscles, César Fuentes had lost his beard and body hair and his voice had turned soprano.

After that, Jacinto tried to be a good friend to César Fuentes, to encourage him, but César Fuentes turned into a manic-depressive, his officemates called him Cesarina and he (César Fuentes) kept insisting that man was nothing but a shit-factory and if, in a noble attempt to rehabilitate him, Jacinto tactlessly made a reference to women,

23

César Fuentes would reply that woman was a shit-factory too but usually smaller.

The sign, at the door of the cabin, reads: Rest and Recuperation Hut No. 13. And before he enters it (the hut) Jacinto shades his eyes with his right hand like a visor, and can still glimpse Darío Esteban's car, wrapped in a cloud of reddish dust, disappearing over the rim of the ravine. The dust hangs over the valley for some minutes and gradually dissipates in the quiet, transparent atmosphere. He (Jacinto) feels weak but unusually calm, and when he turns around he examines the hut, faced with pine logs, with a (very steep) roof of gray slate shingles. Out back is the well, with the platform for the water tank over it, the switch for the electric motor, and, underneath, the shack for implements and tools. Darío Esteban tells him as he says good-bye, "There's everything you need in the cellar, Jacinto San José, food and fuel enough for six months." The doctor has prescribed, however, two months of uninterrupted rest, and Darío Esteban himself repeats this in the car, as soon as Serafín has started the motor: "In two months, Jacinto San José, you'll be well. This trouble of yours is a garden-variety adding neurosis." Then, as the car rounds the corner, Darío Esteban wraps him up to his eyes in a woollen muffler, makes him rest his head on his shoulder, and tells him gently, "Don't worry about a thing, Jacinto San José; the Company has seen to everything," this is all he says, and Jacinto leans confidingly on his shoulder and closes his eyes because the fibers in the scarf brush his face and irritate them (his eyes). From time to time Darío Esteban asks him, "Are you asleep, Jacinto San José?" Jacinto's

"No, Darío Esteban," emerges in a muffled way through the weave of the cloth, but he (Jacinto) lets himself be driven along and, half an hour later, he hears Darío Esteban's grave voice repeating monotonously, "I want you to get two things firmly engraved on your mind, Jacinto San José, only two things, but please don't forget them. First: Darío Esteban never said 'To breathe for Don Abdón or not to breathe, that is the option'; that is idle gossip to which you should pay no attention, and, second, you people are not adding dollars, or Swiss francs, or ingots, or kilowatt-hours, or blacks, or girls in nightgowns, understand me? You're adding ADDENDS, d'you hear me? I think the matter's perfectly clear." Jacinto tries to say yes, but the muffler serves as a gag and so he merely nods his head and Darío Esteban, who has placed an arm around his shoulders when he notices his effort, squeezes him so hard that Jacinto can feel the mark of the pastoral ring in his flesh, and advises him, "Don't force yourself, Jacinto San José, I know you understand me." Then silence falls between them and Jacinto, despite the scarf and despite his closed eyelids, senses the vertical shapes of the trees and the little bumps in the highway and the noises and the smell of burnt straw in the small towns they pass through, and every little while Darío Esteban asks him, "What do we add in the Company, Jacinto San José?" And he answers foggily, as if from the depths of a well, "Addends, Darío Esteban."

As he peers over the edge of the wellhead he (Jacinto) makes out two shining stripes on the surface of the water and calls "Jacintooo!" and the depths of the well answer "Intooo!" and the ravine also says "Tooo!" and, after the last echo, Jacinto smiles and goes out into the sun, to the front of the hut, on the slope that gently descends to the deepest part of the valley where there is a zigzagging brook with rapid, crystal-clear water, flanked by honeysuckles, willows, and brambles. Beyond it (the brook) the slope rises again and the reddish, clayey soil is covered with small oak trees, light brown in color, which thin out as the slope ascends. Almost on the very top is a line of boulders dripping with the thaw, and the gray of the rocks becomes yellow and black in the cavities and hollows owing to the humidity. In the open spaces grama grass grows in clumps, a violent green in contrast to the red clay. The oak trees on the slope cut off the view to the left, in the great curve of the valley, while on the right they (the trees) become thinner amid a low undergrowth of heather, hawthorn, and flowering furze. Beside the river, the ruins of an old mill with two abandoned millstones, piled one on top of the other, and, a little lower down, a group of beehives with six of the hives set into the dark rock provide (the mill and the beehives) the only note, though very undefined, of company in the narrow, abrupt perspective. Above this last feature (above the beehives), in a clearing about the size of a hectare, where the slope is less steep, the ground has been plowed some time ago and the sun picks out, among the reddish tussocks, deep brushstrokes of black shadows. His world (Jacinto's) ends a little higher up in a thick curtain of young trees planted some ten years previously. (Young trees also rise behind the cabin, cutting off the view on that side.)

Jacinto breathes the air in slowly, in small doses, and

breathes it out again in intermittent hisses, ssssst-ssssst, making the mere act of breathing a conscious one, concentrating all five senses on the effort. But Darío Esteban thinks that he is choking and asks, startled, "Are you too warm, Jacinto San José?" And Jacinto nods yes, which is his fate, and, in view of his gesture, Darío Esteban unwinds the muffler and says, "Why didn't you say so before?" And at the very moment when he (Jacinto) opens his dazzled eyes, Serafín leaves the broad gray highway and takes another narrower gray road and, a quarter of an hour later, another wider white highway and, a little later, another reddish dirt road still narrower than the narrow gray one and, lastly, the path, almost blotted out by thyme and groundberry and once more Darío Esteban says to him, "Don't forget, Jacinto San José, Darío Esteban never said 'To breathe for Don Abdón or not to breathe, that is the option,' and in the Company we do not add Swiss francs, or dollars, or kilowatt-hours, or girls in nightgowns but solely and exclusively addends, engrave that on your mind." Suddenly he (Darío Esteban) leans forward and announces, "We're getting close," and the car winds between gullies and oak thickets and, sometimes, leaves the road to avoid a stone and, at such moments, Darío Esteban murmurs "Careful!" and, as they reach the rim of the ravine, the gray slate roof appears, and the two leafy elms and the platform for the water tank and the shed for the motor standing out against the green of the pines and the red color of the earth. And when Serafín has stopped the car, and Jacinto and Darío Esteban get out, Darío Esteban tries to breathe deeply at the same time as he says, "How I envy you, Jacinto San

José," but he chokes on the pure air of the uplands and it gets trapped in his bronchial passages and makes him cough (he tries to muffle the cough by putting the hand with the ring on it to his mouth) and he turns red and bends over at the waist, with choking and hoarse hawking, and Jacinto gives him respectful pats on the back (first aid) until the attack is over and then Darío Esteban straightens up and gives him the enormous plastic bag with the seeds in it and shows him the straight line traced around the hut, where the ground seems to have been carefully raked, and tells him, "That is where you must plant the hedge, Jacinto San José. The bed has already been prepared; all you have to do is plant it and water it."

But all this happened after Jacinto got dizzy in the office when he wrote zeroes.

Jacinto, at first sight, with his watery blue eyes, gives the impression of being nearsighted (besides being honest) and possibly he is, but this can't be known for sure because, though he never uses glasses, in the office he holds papers so close that he almost brushes them with the tip of his nose, and on Sunday afternoons, which he usually spends playing parcheesi with Doña Palmira, Doña Presenta, his landlady's sister-in-law, and Señorita Josefita, the orphan from the apartment downstairs, he asks her (Doña Palmira) to lower the red-fringed lamp that hangs above the parcheesi board to the point that even the most purblind person could make out the numbers.

When Don Cristóbal, the husband of Doña Presenta, Doña Palmira's sister-in-law, was alive, the one who was put away in the Little Brothers of Don Abdón because he did all his business in bed, they did not play parcheesi because Don Cristóbal was bored by intellectual games and "When I play," he used to say, "it's so as not to have to think, hee, hee, hee" because Don Cristóbal always said "hee, hee, hee" every time he spoke, even though he said no more than two words, and in view of his attitude, they would play horse races and funerals, because Don Cristóbal just loved to play jockey or corpse, the former in particular, and every time he put a broomstick between his legs and ran recklessly up and down the hall, he enjoyed himself like a little boy.

Usually these gatherings broke up prematurely because everyone knew that, what with the emotion, Don Cristóbal's sphincters would loosen up and he would make dirty and wee-wee in his pants and Doña Presenta would have to hurry and take him by the hand to the Little Brothers so that they could change him. And they were so used to him (to Don Cristóbal, hee, hee, hee) that on the day he died it seemed that all their initiative died with him, until, after several weeks of demoralization, Doña Palmira, who was very fond of card games, suggested that they play snap and the one who lost would get the slap.

Doña Presenta was in charge of the slaps, when she wasn't the loser naturally, and every time she announced a punishment she liked to spell out the sentence, sadistically: "Jack!" she would say, and then, while she slapped the victim's hand, she would add, "Jack, jack, under every bed a whack," or "Four, one smack more!" and then she would administer it. Or "Three, whee!" and she would administer it. Or "King! kinging it on the mountain, shooting rockets like a fountain," and she would administer increasingly harder hits on the back of the loser's hand, usually without excessive cruelty, except when "Five! pinch 'em alive!" turned up, for in this case Doña Presenta would pinch the flesh of her victim mercilessly, a regular nun's pinch, really twisting, really hard, until he or she (the victim) would yell, "If you start out like this I won't play!" he or she would yell, but it was something she (Doña Presenta) couldn't control and Jacinto knew it and since Jacinto is a person incapable of sparing himself a pain by spoiling the pleasure of a fellow human, he habitually finished the game, when he lost, with his hand raw and skinned.

Months later, when Señorita Josefita became an orphan, they invited her to come upstairs on Sunday afternoons and, taking advantage of being four, to play a few little games of parcheesi. Señorita Josefita was a bit long in the tooth, though she had kept her figure, and had just started to play with the yellow pieces after three years of strict mourning, because Doña Presenta assured her that yellow was half-mourning. Jacinto, who besides being honest was a man anxious to please, as soon as Señorita Josefita brought up the problem in connection with being an orphan, went to every shop in town looking for black pieces, and as he could not find any of the right size he bought some checkers, but they turned out to be too big for the spaces on the parcheesi board, and as Jacinto is a man who is willing to beat his brains out rather than leave a fellow human in the lurch, he solved the problem by smoking the red pieces with a match before the game started. But with use and handling, the soot wore off and when they were most absorbed in the game, Señorita Josefita would say hysterically, covering her eyes with her skinny fingers, "Jacinto, red, I can see the red, I can't touch them," she would say, and Jacinto would patiently take the box of matches out of his vest pocket and smoke up the piece again and Señorita Josefita would smile at him, and when Señorita Josefita smiled the crow's feet at the corners of her eyes would deepen, but Jacinto, who besides being honest is a nice-minded man, did not infer from this that she was old but that her skin was as soft and delicate as cigarette paper.

Often, when Doña Palmira observed these signs of goodness, she would exclaim, "Pray, what kind of a nest have you fallen from, Master Jacinto?" Jacinto had possibly heard this exclamation three or four thousand times, but he didn't realize how much it meant until César Fuentes (nicknamed Cesarina) told him one afternoon down by the river, in the same high-pitched voice as Doña Palmira's, when he (Jacinto) was trying, once more, to rescue him from his frustration, "Pray, what kind of a nest have you fallen from?" César Fuentes asked him, and from that moment onward, Jacinto began to consider the possibility of having fallen from a nest and even asked himself in the mirror about the places he might have fallen from. Doña Palmira was of the same opinion as César Fuentes, or rather César Fuentes was of the same opinion as Doña Palmira, who every time that Jacinto watered the plants or crumbled bread on the balcony for the sparrows, would tell him, "Oh, Master Jacinto, what a fine world you've fallen into!" or perhaps "You're too good for these times." And Jacinto, though he generally attributed Doña Palmira's expressions to the sentimentality arising from frustrated motherhood characteristic of warm-hearted sixty-year-old spinsters, began to doubt, and even to believe that he might well have fallen into the world like a meteorite without anyone inviting him and, what was worse, without anyone expecting him.

But, despite having the conviction that he was no meteorite's child, since the names of his father and mother appeared in the Civil Register, Jacinto could not remember them, and the parenthesis after their names with the word "deceased" seemed like extra surnames to him, like an additional shade of meaning. Of his earliest childhood, Jacinto barely retained a fleeting image of a warm, protective human abundance, a broad rapidly moving thigh which in certain bursts of affection would press him vigorously against its opulent breasts and call him "sweetheart" and "sunshine" (ever since, those expressions have contained for Jacinto, along with the sense of security he yearns for, the quintessence of disinterested love). Doña Palmira explained that as regards abnegation, quite aside from their richness in milk, there is nothing like Galician wet nurses, and the fact is that she, the warm and protective opulence, gave him his milk and years later the news, "Your mummy and daddy, sweetheart, died together, electrocuted in a bathtub."

My, what a hurry they were in! Isn't that right, Jacinto? They must have had to go to the theater or something. (Jacinto opens his eyes wide, wrinkles his forehead, touches his cheeks, and the mirror gives back his lackluster im-

32

age. His naked face makes him feel sad. He scrutinizes himself minutely.)

You're a rare bird, Jacinto, don't tell me you're not, it's anybody's guess what kind of a nest you fell out of, just look at other men your age: married and with a home to maintain. Sure, I know, I'll bet you think I'm dumb, Jacinto, I know you all right, I'll say I do, what ails you is that you're scared, don't pretend, you're scared and that's all there is to it, and by not taking the plunge what you want to avoid is having a son like you, so hesitant and cowardly, or like Gen not to put too fine a point on it, no matter how often you say that Gen's happy because he has gone beyond the rational complex of thinking about the fly, you wouldn't like to have a son like Genaro, now would you? because Genaro may have solved all his problems, he doesn't have to worry about food or what people will say, and on top of that he's in no shape to think about the fly and he doesn't have any responsibilities either, his job's a cinch, you can say anything you want, Jacinto, but just the same don't kid yourself, you wouldn't like to have a son like Gen, admit it, all day long stretched out in the shade of the larch tree, a real lazybones, no matter how you look at it he doesn't do anything but pee and beg a crust of bread and a pat from the first one to pass by. So we're agreed about that, if you had to choose between Genaro and Amando García you'd take the one in the middle, that's logical, he's quite a guy is Amando, professional gelder or whatever you want to call him, just try to choose between the gelder and the geldee and you'll come up with another tie, Jacinto, you wouldn't like it much if you had a son like César Fuentes, there he is, spoiled for all practical purposes, neither fish nor flesh, it isn't as if he were a hermaphrodite,

33

*I'll bet he wishes he were, those are beyond good and evil,
just look at Don Abdón . . . But anyone can tell a mile off
what's wrong with you, Jacinto, you know perfectly well,
the matter with you is that you're scared, just plain scared,
but no matter how scared you are, the world's not going to
change because you're scared; whether you like it or not that's
the way the world is, Jacinto, you can take that for granted,
and if you're frightened by Amando García's hazing tricks,
or the King of Clubs or the Target at the Fair, it's not because they're nasty practical jokes but because, my boy, your
watch has stopped, as they say, you haven't developed, for
heaven's sake, Jacinto, you're getting effeminate, believe me,
you've got to toss those scruples overboard, because if the
law waits for little girls to turn into women before they can
get married and have children, you're not going to get anywhere by waiting until women stop being women to set up a
household without children, Jacinto, you stubborn sonofa-
gun, that's going against nature, hear me? and on the other
hand Señorita Josefita, as fine a person as she is, isn't going
to do you any good either, Jacinto, what you want are security breasts, and she doesn't have a thing along those lines,
I should say not! security breasts, what more could we all
want, I'll say, fearsaving breasts, just like when we were
children, exactly like that, why keep asking for more, Jacinto, that was all over when you were weaned, there isn't
any more, the world has gone around a lot of times since
then, and after all, babies are born every day, so what law
keeps you from breeding some, this panic of yours is ridiculous, Jacinto, and it doesn't lead to anything, I'm telling you,
because everything has its risks and children are more risky
than some other things, obviously, you're telling me, that's*

34

always been true, there's that statue in the hall Laocoön and his sons devoured by serpents, how about that, as if it were nothing, I realize that, but like it or not, life is like that, Jacinto, life is that, either you devour or you're devoured and if you teach your children not to devour you're teaching them to be victims, what a joke that is, and if you teach them to devour you're bringing them up to be executioners, and that's no bargain either, Jacinto, I have to admit it.

All living things moved Jacinto to compassion. On Saturdays, for they had a five-and-a-half-day week in the office, he would keep the top slice from his sandwich in his raincoat pocket and at noon he would go to the lake in the park where swans, peacocks, ducks, pigeons, and sparrows crowded the banks, and, once among them, Jacinto would give a special whistle, whee-whoo-whee, and, in a few seconds, he would be surrounded by all the fauna in the neighborhood. His shrinking figure was so innocuous that pigeons and sparrows perched fearlessly on his head and shoulders looking for their share and he would smile, take the piece of bread out of his pocket, smile, and murmur, "Come on, come on, take it easy, there's enough for all of you," he would smile and proceed to crumble it on the ground but, when he had finished, he was stricken by the imploring looks of the timid birds, who hadn't succeeded in picking up so much as a crumb. This led him (Jacinto) to spend the last Wednesdays of the month with the birds, and so, on those days, when he left the office, he would buy a two-kilo loaf and crumble it on the sidewalk by the pond. The sparrows, with their tiny agility, cheep-chissis, would catch the crumbs almost in the air, while the ducks

35

and peacocks, self-important with their corpulence, scared off the pigeons with their flapping wings, whirr-whirr, pigeons whose infinitely sad cooing, roor-r-r, made Jacinto want to cry, and to prevent this, he (Jacinto) would turn round and round, make a little run and suddenly return, jump, climb on a bench, trying every way he could to scare off the stronger birds and outwit the smarter ones, but, no matter what he did, the snow-white pigeons, roor-r-r, got nothing to eat and Jacinto realized that he would get nowhere by increasing the size of the loaf just to share out more bread among the same birds, but that the problem lay in putting a stop to the insatiable avidity of the strong and crafty ones, for, without doing something to stop the strong and crafty ones, the weak ones would never eat at all, he told himself, and this made him melancholy and a bit distressed and he thought about it in his room, as he watered the begonia, the sansevieria, and the ficus. There was no competition among plants because each and every one of them had a piece of ground, a bed to take root in (he thought) and he (Jacinto) watered them daily, late in the afternoon, and, after that, he would go into ecstasies over the varied vein patterns of the begonia, the stiff leaves with their yellow borders, erect as swords, of the sansevieria and the fanciful indented architecture of the ficus. And if Doña Palmira came in and found him in a reverie, she would chide him maternally, "Watering plants is a job for young ladies, Master Jacinto. Pray, what kind of a nest have you fallen from?"

The dirt soaks up the water with an avid, soothing hissing noise, sssst, like combustion, and when the first puddles begin to form Jacinto shuts off the tap, rolls up the hose, and hangs it on the fork formed by the trunk of the elm tree and a sawed-off branch. The sun is setting now and the evening breeze begins to be noticeable, but, before he goes inside, Jacinto breathes in the air two or three times, in little whiffs, and lets it escape intermittently, in wavering whistles, whew-whoo-whew. In the twilight, two turtledoves fly over his head like two bluish streaks, in the direction of the grove. Back in the hut, Jacinto lights the kerosene lamp, takes a book from the shelf, and sprawls in an armchair with his feet close to the fireplace. "You're out of shape, Jacinto," he (Jacinto) tells himself. He is sure that the exercise has been moderate and yet he feels tired. That morning he has gone down to the mill and bathed his feet in the ice-cold stream, frightening the fugitive trout that swim among the stones on the bottom or the willow branches trailing from its banks. In the afternoon, Jacinto plants the hedge around the hut, mixing the seed with dry earth in equal quantities, just as he had been advised to do, and, to finish the job, gently raking the surface of the displaced earth. Then he screws the hose into the tap of the trough, beside the well, and slowly and deliberately waters the strip he has planted. The day-long silence and solitude have comforted him. Only the vultures, silently taking off from the rocks opposite him, the smaller vulture spying on the grove from overhead or the rabbits' little white scuts popping out from behind the oak trees as he passes, have given him (Jacinto) a vague sensation of living things around him. Apart from this and the splashing of the brook, slap-slap, the cawing of the rooks,

37

kaa, and the sporadic concerts of blackbirds, tchink-tchink-tchink, and nightingales, chook-chook-piu-piu-piu, the silence is total. Now he is very much at home here, a book in his hand which he has no intention of reading (a book held in reserve), the nape of his neck resting on the back of the armchair and, on the hearth, the crackling fire, pff-ptt, which he (Jacinto) feeds from time to time by tossing an oak log on the flames. From his armchair he can see all the inside of the cabin, only one room, which the bookshelves divide conventionally into two: the living room, large and comfortably furnished, and the bedroom, with twin beds, across from which two doors give access to the toilet (gentlemen) and the kitchen with its tiny gas stove where Jacinto has prepared his first meal (soup and meatballs) and whose window opens onto the elms and the well at the back. The ceiling, faced with tigerwood boards, seems to protect his solitude, as do the pictures, books, curtains, and the sable antelope's head with its shining eyes and sharp (double) set of horns that hangs on the chimney piece. Before this Jacinto has toured the places for provisions, the pantry and cellar, and, as he does so, tears come to his eyes and his lips murmur, like a prayer, "Don Abdón is the most motherly father of all fathers." There is no lack of anything there, and this abundance seems like a guarantee of survival. And each time that he finds a new kind of soup, unsuspected rows of tin cans in a corner of the storeroom, enormous boxes of presliced bread protected by plastic bags or the bottles of gas for the stove, the heater, or the refrigerator, Jacinto rubs his hands together and feels a sudden desire to urinate (peace and independence have a very diuretic effect on Jacinto). However, one thing has tarnished his peace of mind while he was preparing his meal on the kitchen stove: as he shaped the meatballs he became dizzy.

As he finished off the eighth zero, Jacinto observed the first symptoms: a fathomless mist before his eyes, a sudden tightening of his stomach and, immediately afterward, nausea. He (Jacinto) lifted the pen from the paper and tried to close up the zeroes more slowly, but the result, though gradual and longer delayed, was exactly the same. Then he tried with the sixes, the eights, and the nines, and with a certain puzzlement discovered that the closed curves of these numbers did not upset him at all, but, when he tried once more with the zero, the dizziness returned, he (Jacinto) felt as if a lizard were running up and down his spine (this could be the end, he said to himself), the sweat running from his armpits while his head filled with confusion. Now the mere fact of looking at zeroes frightened him, to such a degree that he closed his eyes and fanned himself with a stack of pamphlets, but the indisposition continued and the sense of instability made him feel indifferent to everything. He got up awkwardly and, stumbling and leaning on his office-mates' desks, went into the toilet (gentlemen), filled the washbowl to the top and plunged his head and face under water, but, as he emerged, he was shivering and his teeth were chattering, nnnnnnn. A waxen wavering face looked back at him from the mirror, and Jacinto implored it *go on, Jacinto, don't be a fool, if only she'd pick you up, you're sick, gosh, what a face, you look like death warmed over, my God! you poor guy, but ask her please, huh? to pick you up and hug you till she squeezes out all this cold you've got inside. Don't worry about Darío Esteban, he won't say anything, what could he say, if you're sick, what a mess, just imagine if you turn out to be no good for adding, I'd like to know what you'd do then, Darío Esteban has said it himself any number of times: all the great undertakings in history have been made by adding. Everything by dint of adding, adding whatever's available, it doesn't matter what, but if you can't add, you'll turn into a no-good, Jacinto, believe me, I'd like to know what you'd turn your hand to then, you tell me, and if you lose your job the serpents will devour you, that's for sure, just look at Laocoön. Make an effort, go on, don't be a fool, and ask her, ask her to pick you up and hug you, just like when you were a little fellow, remember? "Go to sleep, sweetheart," like a featherbed, what security! Go on, go on, have some, you and everybody else, my boy, you aren't asking for much, I should say not, and maybe Doña Palmira is right, that she was a Galician and Galicians make a lot of milk, Jacinto, just from drinking beer. Sure, I understand, to ask her again to pick you up is asking a lot, because when all's said and done, Jacinto, Galician wet nurses used to leave their poor babies back there for the serpents to devour and they came here so the serpents' children could devour them, get it? That's why you have to ask her humbly, please, and as soon as she holds you tight, as tight as can be, and squeezes all the cold out of your body, then you must tell her, "Thank you, ma'am, and excuse me for what happened."*

He wet his lips with the tip of his tongue and passed his fingers over his eyelids, and as soon as the nausea subsided, Jacinto bent over the tap and drank two big mouthfuls of water, rested his forehead on the mirror and stayed there for a while without moving, comforted by the coolness of its surface, trying to restrain his panting breath. Back at his desk, by the big window (from which he could see Don Abdón every morning teasing Gen:

"Doggy catch, mustn't snatch!"

with the rim of a slice of ham or the skeleton of a partridge), he felt better; he changed the crown nib for a Renaissance nib and licked it gently before he dipped it into the inkwell. With his left hand thrust under his unbuttoned shirt, he (Jacinto) brought his nose down until it was almost touching the paper, trying to stabilize his insides by accustomed actions, and so was able to round off his zeroes without impediment, but, on the third zero of the second addend, his nausea returned worse than ever (the vertigo was so violent that Jacinto squeezed his eyelids together as hard as he could and instinctively clutched at the desktop, while his stomach contracted like a squeezed sponge and saliva rushed into his mouth). After a few seconds, he rose from his seat and appeared before Darío Esteban's wooden minaret like a sleepwalker and "What's the matter with you, Jacinto San José?" said Dario Esteban when he saw him, "You don't look so good," and, as he tried to explain, Jacinto could feel his sluggish tongue and the cold sweat on his forehead freezing his ideas, but he said, merely said, "I get dizzy when I write zeroes, Darío Esteban; it's a strange thing," that's what Jacinto San José said and the other man, Darío Esteban, looked at him with a shade of

41

mockery in his eyes, on his indolent full-moon face, and asked, "It wouldn't be curiosity to know what you're adding, Jacinto San José?" and Jacinto, submissively, "That's all forgotten, Darío Esteban, I assure you," and added with an effort, "I can manage the sixes and nines, even the eights, Darío Esteban, just imagine, even if they are so curvy, no problem, it's only with the zeroes," and during all this Darío Esteban was observing him and nodding and then he said, "All right, all right. And you hadn't noticed anything until today, Jacinto San José?" and "Nothing, Darío Esteban," answered Jacinto, but Darío Esteban had already interrupted him saying, "Excuse me," and focused his binoculars on the west wing of the office, adjusted them, pushed button 83 on his interminable keyboard, pressed the lever of the dictaphone and in a velvety but authoritarian voice said into the microphone, "Number 83, kneel facing the wall; we don't come here to talk, did Number 83 hear me?" and immediately Number 83, Ernesto Blanco, Number 83, knelt down docilely when he received the message through his earphones, while Darío Esteban, on his logwood desk, filled out the form in his impeccable Carolingian calligraphy and, when he had finished filling it out, held it toward Jacinto and told him, "Jacinto San José, take this to the Don Abdón Dispensary, you know where it is, on the corner of Don Abdón Avenue; they'll take care of you."

The doctor tells Jacinto to strip to the waist, to lie down on the table; he examines his right eye with a magnifying glass, explores his chest, makes him sit on the table with his legs dangling, puts something resembling a

42

compass in the bend of his elbow (after winding a rubber thing around his arm) and, finally, hits him three times on the kneecap with a little toy hammer, and Jacinto's leg, helpless and unsupported, gives three kicks in the air, in space, and Jacinto, frightened by his lack of control, smiles and murmurs confusedly, "Excuse me, doctor; I'm not doing it on purpose."

The doctor continues his very careful examination in silence, imperturbable and inscrutable, unhurriedly, and at last, without looking at him, asks in an impersonal voice:

"Symptoms?"

"What?" asks Jacinto.

"Tell me what you feel."

"All right," explains Jacinto. "When I write zeroes I get dizzy; that's all."

The doctor is using his questions the way he used the little toy hammer before, in short, dry bursts.

"How many zeroes?"

Jacinto shrugs his shoulders.

"It depends," he says.

"It depends. What does it depend on?"

"I don't know, on the circumstances," says Jacinto.

"Are there times when you have to write more zeroes than others before you get dizzy?"

"That's right."

"How many times have you gotten dizzy writing zeroes?" asks the doctor impatiently.

"To be exact, the first time I'd been working for half an hour and I figure . . ."

"Be specific, please."

43

"The first time on the eighth zero and the second time on the fifth."

"Let's see," muses the doctor and holds out a blank prescription pad and a ballpoint pen and adds, "Write zeroes until you get tired."

As he begins to write the string of zeroes, Jacinto smiles stupidly but, as he progresses, he feels the doctor's burning gaze on the nape of his neck and a cold nausea begins to arise in his belly and his hand trembles and he hasn't finished even the sixth zero when the doctor, as he observes the growing tremor in his hand, asks, "Already?"

"No, no," says Jacinto. "It's just like at the dentist, it's enough that you're there . . ."

"Continue," threatens the doctor, who is following the ballpoint's tracings on the paper with concentrated attention.

After a while the doctor stands up, panting.

"This is very surprising," he says. "You're not writing zeroes but O's, had you never noticed that?"

Jacinto raises his head, puzzled, and this simple movement (raising his head) appears to irritate the doctor.

"Yes," he says. "Am I not being clear enough? Look at it any way you like," says the doctor, pointing with his index finger at one of the zeroes on the paper, "look at it any way you like, that's not a zero, it's an O."

Jacinto blinks like a hare surprised on its nest and, with each blink, his innocent blue eyes seem more puzzled. He says in a thin little voice, "And might that be serious, doctor?"

The doctor does not answer, he takes an index card from the table top and says in his turn:

"Age?"

"Forty-four," says Jacinto, and, to ingratiate himself with the doctor, smiles and adds in a humorous tone, "It's a palindrome."

But the doctor keeps on hitting away implacably with his toy hammer:

"Married?"

"No."

"Widower?"

"No."

"Divorced?"

"No."

"Unmarried, then?"

"Yes."

The doctor jots nervously on the index card.

"Sex life regular?"

"What?"

"Sex life?" repeats the doctor.

Jacinto gives a muffled giggle and shrugs his shoulders.

"I don't indulge," he confesses.

"Aha," says the doctor, "so you don't indulge, eh?" and looks deeply into his (Jacinto's) eyes and adds, "Have you noticed that your name ends in an o?"

"Why, that's true, I hadn't even noticed it," agrees Jacinto, intrigued.

"Let's see," says the doctor, and again holds out the prescription pad and the ballpoint. "Write your name there."

Jacinto writes Jacinto and raises his eyes.

"Observe, observe," says the doctor. "Now what difference is there between the o of Jacinto and the zeroes you wrote at the top of the page?"

A frightened smile appears on Jacinto's lips as he compares, and then, still looking at the paper and smiling, he says, "Do you know you're right, doctor? They're exactly the same."

"I'm the one who's to say if they're the same or different," shouted Darío Esteban. "Your duty is to add, you needn't concern yourself with anything else."

He was visibly upset, was Darío Esteban, and his facial expressions and movements, now that he had lost control of himself, plainly showed his indignation. Jacinto had never seen him like this except for the incident with Genaro, months before his demotion, since, under ordinary circumstances, Darío Esteban's reprimands (and his punishments) were characterized by moderation and dignity and his (Darío Esteban's) state of mind was usually a reflection of Don Abdón's which Amando García would announce under his breath as soon as Don Abdón crossed the threshold. "Today old Otis has his mustache turned up" (sign of tolerance) or "Today old Otis has his mustache turned down" (sign of intransigence), and he (Darío Esteban) from his logwood minaret and with his binoculars at his eyes, was in a still better position than Amando García to discover the position of Don Abdón's mustache, but now Darío Esteban, completely losing his head, impervious to reason, began to yell, despite the fact that Jacinto knew for certain that Don Abdón had arrived with his mustache turned up, and, perhaps because of this, perhaps because he thought it was his duty, Jacinto tried to convince Darío Esteban that it would be a good plan to inform the office force about the numbers they were adding, for even though he (Darío Esteban) insisted that all numbers were the same, it was obvious that there were numbers written in red ink and others in green ink, hence they were not the same, and that— added Jacinto—in case he didn't know it, there had been a near-mutiny about this in the Refectory, a few days previously, when one of the clerks (it doesn't matter who) remarked that to add without knowing what you were adding depressed the work force and led to the dissemination of idle rumors since there were those who affirmed that they were dollars and others that they were Swiss francs and others that they were kilowatt-hours (that were being added) and there were even some who suggested that it might be a question of drugs, blacks, or girls in nightgowns (white slave trade) since there were people in the world who dealt in drugs, blacks, and girls in nightgowns, and that the most practical thing—added Jacinto—to stop wagging tongues, would be to inform the office force, since nobody's efficiency would be reduced by identifying the figures that he was adding, and, on the other hand, by correcting this omission some of the clerks' scruples of conscience about thinking that they were adding something horrid would be avoided, and Darío Esteban listened solemnly to all this from atop his wooden minaret and Jacinto thought, "It's as if I'd been wound up like a mechanical toy," and Darío Esteban's face, in the course of his (Jacinto's) speech, turned first yellow, then green, and lastly crimson, and when it seemed that he was on the point of exploding, he opened the door of his pulpit, slid down the banister and, as he landed on the thick carpet, said, "Follow me, Jacinto San José."

Once in the main office, Darío Esteban's right cheek began to boil (bubbles of flesh formed and bounced up and down as if his jowls had started to simmer) and he pronounced an impassioned speech in short bursts of eloquence, accompanied by histrionic gestures, in a tone that alternated between the most unbridled anger and the most imploring abjection (and at these moments his eyes filled with tears), a circumstance which Darío Esteban employed to brandish unanswerable arguments: a) Perpetual debt toward Don Abdón. b) No one in the world ought to receive more money than what he needs for two meals a day, a soccer game every two weeks, and the monthly payments on the television set. To give less would be inhuman; to give more would lead to vice and would, therefore, be equally inhuman, and c) In Don Abdón, Ltd., asking questions was the same as stealing, since Don Abdón paid people for adding and not for asking questions.

The mention of Don Abdón, the unanswerable logic of the minimum-maximum salary (which fully demonstrated that Don Abdón was not an overbearing man), the bubbling of Darío Esteban's cheek made Jacinto hesitate, *but Jacinto, you just kept hammering away, and not out of stubbornness, I know it's not that, but because you've never liked to leave things half done, what you begin you finish, ever since you were little, ever since you were so high, and that was when you told him about the confusion, and*

48

the rumors, and the gossip, and he (Darío Esteban) just kept staring at you at eye level, as if he were counting your eyelashes, but he let you talk and when you got it all off your chest, remember? he pulled out a pad of paper and a ballpoint and "Names, names," asking who were the ones who said they were adding kilowatt-hours and who were the ones who said they were adding dollars and who were the ones who said they were adding blacks and who were the ones who said they were adding girls in nightgowns, dammit, he couldn't seem to say anything else, but you, Jacinto, you clammed up, a fine fellow you are, you may have other faults but you're not a tattletale, not a syllable, mum's the word, when you got well under way I thought he (Darío Esteban) was going to have a stroke, Jacinto, you've really got a nerve, I think you didn't even realize what you were saying: "We all have weaknesses, Darío Esteban; remember that you said yourself, one day in the Refectory before they promoted you to monitor: 'To breathe for Don Abdón or not to breathe, that is the option' "; Mother of God, Jacinto, how could you ever have said such a thing, you really are something, if somebody had pricked him (Darío Esteban) just then I'll bet you two to one he wouldn't have bled a drop, imagine, but he hid it, what could he do, after all, it's so important to him, I'll say, he just kept waving the penpoint around, "Names, names," his face was blue, almost black, Holy Virgin! and he kept saying "Names, names," and you cool as a cucumber, Jacinto, as if it was nothing to do with you, just like a condemned man who wants to say everything he thinks before he dies, "I'm asking, Darío Esteban, but if you can't answer me, we'll still be friends, we're not going to quarrel about that, I should say not, you level with me and I'll level

49

with you, I may have other faults but nobody can beat me
for enthusiasm and hard work," and he (Darío Esteban)
wanting to have his cake and eat it too, naturally, trying to
change the subject, sure, first the turned one color (blue) and
then another (red), and he said that if memory served you
had three Adding Prizes, December 1949, March 1962, and
June 1967, some memory, Jacinto, give him his due, with the
number of clerks there are, and if you want to know any-
thing else just ask, he really gilded the pill, that he had no
complaints about your behavior, but he turned the tables on
you, sure, absolute devotion to duty, Carolingian calligraphy
A-plus, but, pretending it wasn't important, that little ques-
tion about what all of you were adding was out of order and
even a little bit subversive, he left you scared to death, Ja-
cinto, rooted to the spot as the saying goes, don't say you
weren't, you were in a great hurry to take it all back, you
seemed like a different person, as if you'd just run out of gas,
hoping that he'd excuse you, that if you asked you'd done so
in good faith, that all you wanted to do was look out for the
prosperity of the Company, Darío Esteban, the sole aim was
to stimulate all of you and he (Darío Esteban) kept scrib-
bling away at a great rate and, when he finished, re-
minded him (Jacinto) that Genaro Martín had been demoted for less, a corrective which, as was to be expected
of Don Abdón's benevolent heart, had turned into an
award because to strip a man of prejudices and responsibilities was the same as opening the doors of paradise
to him.

Jacinto agreed (yes, yes, yes), overwhelmed, ready to
renew his argument and then, for no reason, Darío Esteban asked him point-blank if he was acquainted with

Mr. Darwin's theory of the evolution of species, and Jacinto said superficially, only superficially, and Darío Esteban said that he should note that Don Abdón was not an evolutionist but a revolutionist, that is, that he thought that monkeys came from man and man from monkeys, both were true, that is, that man, after progressing to maximum maturity, was returning to the point of departure, and that the moment of regression seemed to have arrived, and hence, by demoting Genaro Martín he was only aiding his return to more elementary human forms, or rather, to instinctual behavior, or rather, to sum it up in one word, to the state of happiness.

At about noon comma when they got out of school comma Genaro's twin boys comma Pedro Juan and Juan Pedro comma would come galloping along the sidewalk of hexagonal paving blocks comma they streaked through parenthesis grabbing the bars with their right hands close parenthesis the iron gate and said how are you, daddy as they dashed by and comma galloping along the cinder paths among the box and the floral borders comma they came together on the marble staircase comma appeared in front of the concierge's box comma and gasped to Señor Artemio comma the concierge comma the permit for my daddy and comma meanwhile comma Gen comma who had smelled them comma would emerge from the doghouse dragging his chain comma frantically wagging his head from side to side and looking toward the concierge's box with his hazel eyes momentarily alight comma his ears stiff as starched rags comma impatiently wiggling his hairy bottom and comma when he spotted the twins running madly toward him comma waving the permit comma he would get all excited and begin to tug on his chain until he rubbed the skin off his neck and then he would cringe comma bashfully comma waiting until his children changed the clip of the heavy chain for the clip of the flexible leash that his wife had given him for Christmas to go for walks in period Gen felt happy then with the twins frisking around him comma taking turns holding the leash and comma if he happened to squat on the hexagonal paving blocks or snuggle up to a tree or a lamppost and raise his left leg comma they would wait till he finished making water and would laugh happily and say colon Have you noticed what a lot of pee daddy makes now?

Gen's hands and feet had grown protective calluses as his fingers had shrunk comma and his thickened nails curved over them comma coming to a point at the ends like claws period His transformation was general and progressive for comma apart from the thick fuzz that covered his trunk and limbs parenthesis a brown and white fuzz comma speckled comma with random spots comma so thick that you could not see his skin close parenthesis comma his chest became convex while his skinny slippery hips withdrew into the graceful curves of his thighs and comma on the other hand comma his arms and legs became thinner comma although they did not grow weaker comma and on his legs the joints of his kneecaps turned around comma that is comma they bent backward instead of forward period But the twins paid no attention to such trifles comma they would say colon Run, daddy! comma they would say comma and Gen would go tearing off at a wild gallop dragging the boy who was holding the leash and the boy who was holding the leash would yell gasping comma with the wind in his face comma he would shout colon Stop, daddy, please, I'm going to fall! and comma when Gen came to a halt comma all three would pant comma Gen in a faster rhythm parenthesis two or three pants for every one of his children's close parenthesis rolling his bleary eyes and showing a long pink tongue end of paragraph

Once they reached the green belt in the suburbs comma the twins comma exhausted comma would sit down on a creek bank or perch on a culvert and chat comma but Gen comma uninterested in their conversations comma would wander listlessly between them comma he would place his muddy hands on their sweaters or suddenly lick their faces and they would push him away laughing daddy, go lie down! comma they would tell him and Gen comma docilely comma after describing a dozen circles around himself comma examining the ground comma would curl up at their feet end of paragraph

Parenthesis One afternoon when Gen's children were yelling at their father comma as he ran Stop, daddy, please, I'm going to fall! and Gen didn't stop comma Pedro Juan had to let go of the leash and when Gen comma hearing him call comma returned comma Pedro Juan whipped him hard with the end of the leash and Gen accepted the punishment submissively comma squatting comma looking out from under his lashes at him comma his eyes bloodshot comma without making a sound period Juan Pedro scolded his brother for his behavior you hit daddy, Pedro Juan, he told him and at first Pedro Juan was sorry comma but a moment later comma he burst out laughing and it's true, listen, I hit him and he doesn't scold me comma he said and after that every time that Gen disobeyed comma his children would whip him with the leash and Gen's grieving and resigned attitude during the whipping produced unrestrained laughter in them close parenthesis end of paragraph

As soon as they reached open country comma the twins would unfasten the clip so that their father could let off steam by running aimlessly on all fours through fields and pine groves and comma from the top of the bank comma the boys would follow his wanderings comma they watched him come and go comma crawl around comma industriously scratch his back with his foot comma search among the furrows and if accidentally comma guided by smell comma Gen discovered a garbage dump or the remains of a picnic comma he would stop and dig until he found something he wanted to eat and comma in those cases comma he would bend down and gobble whatever it was voraciously comma looking sideways and if the children interrupted him while he was doing this Gen would drive them off showing his canine teeth and they would laugh and remark colon Just look how hungry daddy is now; he even eats bones they would remark end of paragraph

On sunny Sunday mornings Jacinto would go with them but comma unable to adjust his stride to Gen's and the children's comma he would lag behind meditating and comma sometimes comma he would turn on his transistor period At first he tried to converse seriously with Gen but he never got any other reply than a howl or a lick on the face and comma considering these failures comma Jacinto decided to buy the transistor because it depressed him to see Gen running hither and yon for hours through the open fields and he thought that the Sunday morning program of EAV 83 the Voice of Don Abdón comma the local broadcasting station comma would hold his attention since he had been crazy about operettas since childhood period And indeed comma the first time that Gen heard one of the well-known choruses comma he curled up at Jacinto's feet and stayed perfectly still next to the radio with his eyes half-shut comma until the program was over comma but the following Sunday the music hardly kept Gen quiet for more than a quarter of an hour and comma after that comma it was a rare occasion when Jacinto succeeded in getting Gen to lie down for more than a minute comma for a flock of sheep or a horse or a motorcycle passing along the road was enough to make him dash off furiously asking for water comma wa-wa-wa comma at the top of his voice period Jacinto was alarmed by Gen's growing indifference to things that until then had entranced him and his alarm increased on the morning that he found on the lower end of Gen's spinal column comma just over the anus comma a hairy protuberance end of paragraph

This was the beginning of Gen's profound psychic transformation comma for when spring arrived his ecstasies began accompanied by paralysis and sudden attacks of excitement period Now it was no longer merely flocks of sheep comma motorcycles and horses comma but children and poultry who made Gen beside himself comma hens particularly excited him so much that comma despite the fact that Jacinto called to him and threatened him comma Gen would not obey until he saw the hens fleeing in hasty confusion over the barnyard walls period But all this was nothing compared to the attacks comma the fits of derangement and convulsive trembling brought on by very unimportant things comma which Gen began to suffer from in the early days of May period The first attack happened when Gen was running happily through a potato field with his nose to the ground as was his custom and comma suddenly comma without knowing why or why not comma he stopped comma remained perfectly still comma rigid as a stick comma his trembling body slightly arched comma stiff-legged comma his hazel eyes fixed on a plant comma his slavering mouth half open comma as if he were smiling and Jacinto comma when he saw him like that comma ran toward him and tried to bring him back to himself by stroking his back and speaking to him tenderly Gen don't be so foolish Don't you feel well? comma but Gen comma unreachable comma neither heard his words nor felt his petting semicolon he just stared and trembled and stayed like that for several minutes until he suddenly gave a leap comma his hands together comma as if he were trying to catch something comma nervously comma and from between his fingers comma near his nose comma a partridge flew out with a short whistle whic-whic period Jacinto sighed are you being stupid, Gen? it's only a bird comma he repeated comma but Gen ran disappointedly crosswise of the furrows until the partridge hid behind an almond tree comma but after that Gen's visions became more frequent and on each occasion comma he was more and more carried away with the peculiarity that a shrew or a lark or a weasel was enough to bring them on comma and his strange behavior became even more marked in the presence of a cocker bitch whose owner comma the director of the Don Abdón Bank comma took her out every Sunday for a stroll among the pine groves period The bitch impressed Gen so much that he never left her side comma he lay in wait for her comma he frisked around her comma he became absorbed in watching her comma his eyes feasting on her comma his ears floppy comma watching her least movement period And the director of the Don Abdón Bank would say colon Look out! you'd better tie him up; the bitch was just coming into heat comma but Gen went up close to her comma sniffed her behind and the bitch smelled his behind and the children chorused delightedly they've made friends, they've made friends! comma they shouted comma and Jacinto Gen, come here! comma but Gen and the bitch kept on smelling each other until the director of the Don Abdón Bank gave the bitch a kick and the bitch started off at a mad run through the market gardens and Gen ran after the bitch and Jacinto ran after Gen and the twins ran after Jacinto and comma at this point comma the farmer appeared and yelled semicolon Can't you see you're fucking up my field! comma but the bitch had already stopped at the edge of the field and Gen next to her sniffing her and Jacinto next to Gen and the twins next to Jacinto comma while the director of the Don Abdón Bank whistled twee-twee from the other side of the cabbage plants and Jacinto comma in view of the

57

difficulties comma tied Gen up and pulled on the leash with all his might and Gen and the cocker bitch kept staring at each other the whole time and after he reached the end of the furrow comma Gen turned stubborn and refused to drink water comma he didn't even try to please Jacinto comma and Jacinto comma cautiously comma warned the twins comma he warned them not a word about this to mama, hear? comma then he tied Gen up comma took off his jacket and lay down comma his hands behind his head comma in the dappled shade of the poplars comma profoundly vexed end of paragraph

It is excessively hot in the sun and too cold in the shade, for there is a sharp mountain breeze, and in view of these alternatives Jacinto places the easy chair in the half-shade of the elm tree, next to the well, a couple of meters behind the shed for the motor and the tool shack. There is a silence which the chirping of the sparrows, cheep-chissis, and the whistles of the blackbirds, tchink-tchink-tchink, and the cooing of the turtledoves in the pine grove, roo-coo, makes even deeper. And in the intervals, whenever the birds stop singing, the murmur of the rapids in the river wearing away the stones, slap-slap, making the willows that trail from the banks wave gently, reaches him (Jacinto). Jacinto has his transistor at hand but makes no move to turn it on. He is tired in spite of having slept and the vague memory of lying half-asleep brings back to his mind, without his volition, the nightingale's nocturnal song as it waited for its eggs to hatch, piu-piu-piu-chook-chook. He raises his eyes looking for the nest among the elm branches but can only find, almost at the top, the elementary stick-and-rubble web of an old magpie's nest. Suddenly, at the base of the tree, he (Jacinto) spies the treecreeper climbing up the bark in a spiral with its skinny legs, and scarcely has it (the treecreeper), teet-teet, reached the lowest branches than it flies off and comes to rest on the shed for the motor, looks doubtfully (the treecreeper) from side to side, and finally slips into a crack between two boards. Jacinto smiles faintly. The bird stays hidden for a few seconds behind the logs of the cabin and finally reappears only to fly (in an irregular flight, with long swoops) tee-teroi-titt, toward the grove of young trees on the slope. "It's making a nest," he (Jacinto) says to himself, and turns his gaze down the hill, over heather and furze, until it rests on the ruined mill, on whose remains a pair of partridges are taking the sun, motionless as stones, and then it (Jacinto's gaze) climbs up the other side of the valley, among the oaks and patches of grama grass, to the rocky gray garland with its blackish-yellow hollows, over which the vultures are flying. When it reaches the summit, it (Jacinto's gaze) returns, takes in the head of the valley farther to the north, slides gently over the oak thicket still in winter leaf, takes the path and reaches the cabin: Rest and Recuperation Hut No. 13.

Obviously the hut is of recent construction. There, at his feet, around the well, the cement crust, strewn with chips of stone and brick, with kindling and chunks of newly-sawed logs, holds back the underbrush. As he continues to look around him Jacinto's glance encounters the gate made of pine logs, totally superfluous because access to the cabin is open on all four sides. "They must have built it with the hedge in mind," he (Jacinto) tells himself aloud and before he has finished saying it he sees that the hedge is already in existence and his (Jacinto's) stomach contracts, and his (Jacinto's) heart speeds up, tick-tack-tick, as though in the presence of a marvel and he stands up and then he verifies the fact that the rectangle around the hut is turning green although scarcely fourteen hours have elapsed since he planted the hedge and twelve since he watered it. "It's not possible," he tells himself, and, immediately, he squats down and verifies that here and there the reddish earth is breaking up, and through the tiny cracks tender greenish-white shoots are appearing and his astonishment increases when he concentrates his attention on one of them (the shoots) and sees it produce a short but perceptible spurt of growth, just as one can, by watching them very insistently, see the hands of an old tower clock move in intermittent jumps. "Why, I'm watching it grow," he (Jacinto) tells himself, frightened, almost screaming, and the ravine answers, "Row," and Jacinto, as if the mountain were being sarcastic, repeats defiantly "Yes, grow!" and the ravine answers more loudly "Row!" but Jacinto says no more, observing the ground bubbling (as if a hundred moles were simultaneously digging under the surface), the fissures opening up in the strip that was flattened yesterday by the water, the whitish sprouts that appear in them like little animals, the dark buds, rough and green, at their ends, just about to burst.

His right leg, half-hidden among the three legs of the stool, goes to sleep, and Jacinto surreptitiously stretches it from time to time so as not to distract Don Abdón, who is undoubtedly gratified to have him nod assent each time he pauses, and so, when Don Abdón asks him if he is timid, Jacinto bows his head in recognition of his timidity and, incidentally, relieves the tightness in his neck and frees his first cervical vertebra from the weight of his head. Jacinto cannot remember a moment of greater confusion. Don Abdón, sitting crosslegged, his turgid breasts bare, framed by the Solomonic columns of the golden baldachin, appears to his fascinated eyes like a god before whom the only possible reaction is acquiescence. The winged, chubby-cheeked children in the cupola, mute witnesses of the interview, seem to infuse wisdom into Don Abdón, who pronounces the dictum "The hedge is the defense of the timid," in a total voice which soaks into Jacinto through his ears, through his nostrils, through his eyes, through his mouth, and through each one of his pores, and which causes Jacinto, completely intimidated, to nod his head again and when Don Abdón takes up his speech, after another short pause, Don Abdón is by now an absolute presence whose voice descends from the cupola, from the thick walls, surrounding him, penetrating him, soaking him (Jacinto) like fog or a persistent shower of rain: "Only a short time ago your illness would have meant a catastrophe, but nowadays the Company foresees these contingencies, for in the new order man has ceased to be an instrument," that is what Don Abdón says and Jacinto lowers his head, his eyes magnetically attracted to the black nourishing nipples, completely cowed by the silent inhabitants of the cupola, by the legions of scribes, copyists, and clerks on the walls who busy themselves with complicated arithmetical operations. From below,

61

from the humble stool, Don Abdón seems to Jacinto—
squatting like a Buddha, his thrusting breasts bare—more
father, more mother, more important, more domineer-
ing, more transcendent than in any other circumstance
of his life. And when Don Abdón takes the white card
in his hands and tells him, "Protected by the hedge you
will be able to think deeply," Jacinto knows immediately
what he is talking about. The photocopy that Amando
García gave him two months ago reads exactly as follows:

> Jacinto San José Niño, born 17 October 1924. Entered 23
> June 1942. Hardworking, obedient and disciplined clerk.
> Adding Prizes fourth quarter of 1949, first quarter of 1962
> and second quarter of 1967. Calligrapher of the first class.
> Confused Christian. Hobbies: books about the sea, par-
> cheesi, plants, and birds. Resistant to soccer, television,
> and religious holidays. Sentimental and with humanitar-
> ian prejudices. Interceded for Genaro Martín in 1953. In
> May 1966 evinced an unhealthy curiosity about the ulti-
> mate reasons for his work. Covers up for a number of of-
> ficemates who ask improper questions. Has no faith in
> words. In 1956 founded the movement Through Silence to
> Peace, taken up only in a lukewarm manner by his fellow
> workers. Still believes in man and in a good conscience.
> Under observation."

Jacinto can read this (or guess at it) just from seeing the
back of the card in Don Abdón's hand. And when Don
Abdón's absolute voice fills the room with echoes, Jacinto shudders; habituated to the great silence in a few
seconds, he rises fervently and, seeing the outstretched
hands with the dark plastic bag of seeds, he stands up,
ascends step by step, while the lofty cupola, the apse,

the niche, and the thick walls repeat, in cavernous inter-mingled echoes: "Don't forget about the hedge. Here are the seeds. It's an American hybrid that proliferates in a very short time. Biology has never before achieved such marvels." Jacinto takes the bag awkwardly, over-whelmed by the proximity of the white nourishing breasts, the shining columns of the baldachin, the child trumpeters, the emptiness of the immense room that roars in his ears like a spiral seashell, but he takes the bag and mumbles, "Thank you, Don Abdón," he mumbles, steps slowly backward and, when he reaches the stool, feels for it with his right foot so as not to trip and continues to walk backward, with the huge bag clutched to his chest and making bows, and Don Abdón and his hospitable breasts gradually recede, until Jacinto's behind bumps against the mahogany door and, then, with his left fore-arm, he presses the bag against his chin and puts the other hand behind him, fumbles for the doorknob, opens the door and goes out after making a last and abject bow.

When he returns from the mill, Jacinto observes that a number of the buds have flowered. "Oh, God! Where is this going to end?" he (Jacinto) tells himself. He sets the basket with the remains of his lunch in it down at the door and sits on the ground, near the gate. He (Jacinto) is startled. The most precocious plants are now five cen-timeters off the ground and some are standing upright and others are growing sideways and others are crawling among the cement blocks. His attention is drawn in so many directions that he doesn't know where to look. The plants are still fragile and, in most of them, the buds are closed or half open, but in some the flowering is complete, the single bloom lying limply in two sections, four fingers on one side and another wider one on the other, like a vegetable hand. In the little flowers six stamens, with very fine filaments and prominent anthers, covered with a sticky yellow dust, appear timidly, as if in miniature. Jacinto bends down, brings his nose very close to the sprouts, never tires of looking at them. The bright yellow of the anthers begins to fade in the filaments only to vanish in the corolla which, in its turn, connects with the green stem in an imperceptible chromatic transition. Under the flower sprout the first leaves, minute but complete in shape. Looking at those leaves gives Jacinto the same wondering emotion as looking at the tiny nails on the little fingers of newborn babies. The upper surfaces are an explosively bright green and contrast with the under sides, which are dull and look as if they had been powdered. They remind Jacinto of ilex leaves, so stiff, strong, and many-veined. He (Jacinto) is fascinated, in the clutch of a nervous tremor. He stares at a mature bud, slender and long as a match, and observes how its end turns rusty in a few seconds, acquires the color of tobacco and, immediately afterward, opens (after a brief crackling noise, crrick, it seems to Jacinto) and allows the stamens to stand up like little worms, and simultaneously the petals fall off, lose their erection, wrinkle and wither. The freshness of the new flower masks the withering of the petals. "My God, my God!" says Jacinto, who has stood up when he noticed that the pavement is making his bottom cold. Now he gazes along the lateral strip (in a straight line from the log gate) and slowly walks around all four sides of the hedge. On all of them the red

64

earth is cracking around the vertical stems, and new shoots are appearing in every fissure. It is a general and uniform invasion of irresistible force. Jacinto's astonishment is evidenced by his sudden exclamations, by the tremulous delicacy with which he gently touches the fragile stems, by the tenderness with which he examines the filaments of the yellow flowers. When he finishes his inspection he makes two more turns around the hut before deciding to take the hoe and dig another strip half a meter wide next to the one he has already planted. "I must make a strong hedge," he tells himself. "Don Abdón is going to be surprised; it's even more prolific than he can imagine," he tells himself, while his shirt becomes soaked with sweat and he (Jacinto) digs and digs fervidly, without a pause, for once without noticing his body and by the time the sun is low over the hill Jacinto has turned it over and raked it all. "Tomorrow I'll plant it," he says to himself with secret pleasure before entering the cabin. Suddenly he feels cold, he shuts the door and lights the log fire, the lamp, the heater, and the kitchen stove. He is aware of a faraway moan, wheee, in his trachea as he exhales and asks himself, "What's that?" he asks himself, looking at his reflection in the mirror of the toilet (gentlemen), *now don't start being stupid, Jacinto, because you're so hard up here, you haven't anyone to lend you a hand and after all it's not that important, for, really, you haven't done anything but start a hedge, and that's your business, and if Doña Palmira and everybody else think that there's no reason to argue about situations where they can't agree with you, then let them go jump, and if they're right let them take the consequences, what does it* matter to you what Doña Palmira and everybody else say? don't you worry, Jacinto, if you're happy reading a book about the sea or watering a flower, everybody else can go to blazes, see. Sure, I know, I agree, as if I didn't know, what you're doing with all that is sharpening your sensitivity and sensitivity is nothing but an amplifier of pain, whether you decide to be the victim or the executioner, because really there isn't any other choice, either you devour or you're devoured, there's no two ways about it, agreed, but if this satisfies you there's no need to tell the world about it and if Doña Palmira and everybody else think differently, well fine, let them think it, don't you worry, Jacinto. And, for the love of God, don't remind me about Genaro again, Jacinto, for heaven's sake, I don't know why that dratted Genaro matters so much to you but you never stop talking about him, and everything you can possibly tell me about him I know by heart already, everything, so if he lifts his leg next to the larch tree a hundred times a day and you take away the larch tree and put a broomstick in its place, he'll keep on lifting his leg next to the broomstick a hundred times a day without noticing the change, some novelty that is; but even if it were like that, what can you do for him, you tell me, Jacinto? Stop feeling anything, that's just great, I'll say, and what do you eat that with? Huh? Want to give me the recipe? Where do you cut to make yourself stop feeling? It's mighty easy to talk, Jacinto, but things are as they are and it's not enough to know that the man with feelings is the laughingstock of those who don't have feelings, and furthermore, he causes confusion; knowing all that about being a laughingstock and causing confusion isn't enough to make you stop feeling, Jacinto, don't kid yourself, even resorting to words doesn't do you any good;

66

words, now, can you think of a greater reason for confusion? Really the doctor is absolutely right, if you can't tell a zero from an O, why, you hadn't even noticed, Jacinto, admit it, what's so special about the fact that words are confusing and that everyone gives different meanings to the same words? If man's imagination is so weak that he can't manage to invent a squiggle that clearly differentiates the zero from the O, Jacinto, then everything's bound to be confusion, you can be sure of that, because a lot of people are interested in stirring it (confusion) up, because the smart operators get a lot of mileage out of it (out of confusion), see? and the only chance for getting along together that was ever offered to us humans, the Tower of Babel, we threw it away like fools.

Jacinto, whenever he is thinking, rubs his head; he tries to shape his ideas with his hands. It is a great effort for him to work them (the ideas) out and still more to put them (the ideas) in order and still more to get them (the ideas) out in the open because they frequently stick to his brain like tapeworms and only rings come out, while the head stays inside. Maybe all this is a result of timidity, for Jacinto is profoundly, immaculately timid and when, let's say, he goes into church and takes holy water to cross himself with, his initial movement (bringing his thumb to his forehead) is correct but, inevitably, he finishes it with a hasty sketch of a movement because he suspects that the rest of the faithful are watching him. The same thing happens with his genuflections before the high altar: his right knee never brushes the floor and although he always means to do it (make his knee touch the floor) he is prevented by an overwhelming desire to cut the movement short. Let's not even mention the can-

67

ticles (in church), especially if some girl is nearby, in which case Jacinto opens his mouth, puckers or stretches his lips in agreement with the volume of the choir, that is, he presents the picture of someone who is singing but is careful not to emit a single sound. His timidity does not allow him to keep his mouth shut when others have theirs open but neither does it allow him to join with the choir.

Something similar happens if he lends or borrows money, for in both cases Jacinto winds up the loser, since if he lends to someone he is scared to ask for what he is owed and if he borrows he gets terribly embarrassed when he is asked for it. In both cases, as long as the debt remains unpaid, Jacinto tries to avoid the other party (lender or borrower), for if he does encounter him (the other party) and it is he (Jacinto) who has done the lending, he can't bear the thought that the other is thinking that he (Jacinto) is thinking about asking him for the money he owes him, and if it is the opposite case, that is, if he (Jacinto) receives a loan, his embarrassment arises from the thought that the other is thinking that it is time for him (Jacinto) to cough up the money. This leads him, owing to his innate inability complex, to distrust himself and, in principle, to accept as good, with no previous analytical process, all propositions made to him by others.

So Genaro's idea seemed reasonable to him because, by means of a universal language, men from all over the world could at last exchange ideas, mutually improve themselves and, in the end, perhaps understand each other despite their leaders. The Esperanto Group used to meet every Thursday at eight o'clock in the evening at the Don Abdón Academy, and between the "Karaj Kunuloj" with which Genaro opened the sessions and the "Gis morgau, amikoj" with which he dismissed its members, the meetings took place in a conversational and harmonious atmosphere although Genaro tried his best to lead them toward a realistic environment: "Konsideru Ke tie ci Kunestas Kuindek personoj, Kaj la mondo havas pli ol du mil milionoj de logantoju." This and reading the newspaper every morning began to arouse skepticism in Jacinto and, in the course of time, led him to desert the group. Jacinto observed that the more the leaders talked among themselves the more disturbed humanity became, from which he deduced that on the day when a billion and a half men were able to engage in dialogue with a billion and a half others, the world would turn into a madhouse. "This isn't the way to do it," Jacinto told himself one day, but he held his peace for a few weeks because it pained him to hurt his friend's feelings. One afternoon, however, when Genaro was complaining about his (Jacinto's) lack of enthusiasm for the cause, Jacinto answered, "The spoken word is not only undependable but an instrument of aggression," and then Genaro Martín tried to play down Jacinto's argument and, as the ultimate expression of disdain, brought one finger to his forehead and twisted his fingertip pretending to be tightening a screw, but a week later, in the Refectory, amid general stupefaction, Genaro confronted Darío Esteban and told him, "What I say is, Darío Esteban, why instead of so many hospitals and rest and recuperation huts don't they raise our salaries so that we can eat better and that way we'll get sick less often," he told him, and the demand was so sudden that, for the moment, Darío Esteban did not answer, he merely looked at Genaro as if he were measuring him from head to foot, and, at last, he lifted the hand with the ring on it and, pointing vaguely, said, "Go at once to the Visitors' Room, Genaro Martín," and once there, in the Visitors' Room, Darío Esteban exploded. "To hell with logic, Genaro Martín, if your question is meant to be logical; a thinking man ought to be thinking about a bed to die in nobly rather than about eating. I cannot hide from you, Genaro Martín, the fact that your error in the Refectory a few minutes ago is among those which the rules of this Company define as very grievous. What you are doing is to doubt, Genaro Martín, that Don Abdón is the most motherly father of all fathers." And when he said this Genaro Martín got angry, in the Visitors' Room, and that I will not accept, Darío Esteban, he said, that is a principle, not a statement that can be questioned, he said, and Darío Esteban's eyes bored into him, gave off sparks, and his (Darío Esteban's) right cheek began to bubble like a pot of water boiling, and, as the bubbling died down, he said, in the Visitors' Room, "Then tell me, Genaro Martín, who is the Company?" and Genaro Martín, without hesitation, "Don Abdón, Darío Esteban," and Darío Esteban "And who is the Company Rule, Genaro Martín?" and Genaro Martín, without hesitation, "Don Abdón, Darío Esteban," and Darío Esteban, in the Visitors' Room, "Then can you dispute the proposition that order is freedom?" and Genaro Martín, at this point, hesitated, cleared his throat, and "Not at all, Darío Esteban," he said at last and, as the bubbling decreased in Darío Esteban's right cheek, his arguments—Darío Esteban's—became imbued with a certain amount of serenity and "With your logical mentality, Genaro Martín, you must understand," he said, "that to question the Company Rule, which is Don Abdón, involves disorder and all disorder, consequently, once that premise is admitted, involves an attack on freedom," that's what Darío Esteban said, all in one breath, and his chest (Darío Esteban's) swelled as he finished his speech, while Genaro Martín answered, in a choked voice, brushing a bit of invisible dust off the lapel of his coat, "If you understand it like that, Darío Esteban, I beg your pardon," but it was too late and the full-moon face of Darío Esteban waggled from side to side and Darío Esteban adopted his baritone voice to state, "The wrong is irreparable, Genaro Martín, and as monitor I have no choice but to fire you."

For weeks Genaro Martín wandered through the city like a leper, begging from door to door, but the doors, without exception, were closed to him and the Group expelled him from its bosom and his officemates crossed the street to avoid speaking to him and people said, "He's a revolutionary, he asks questions when the answers have already been given," and other people said, "Anyone else (but Don Abdón) would have beaten him up and kicked him out of the city," and other people said, "He's a hyena; he has bitten the hand that fed him." In those weeks of hardship Genaro Martín received visits only from Jacinto, despite the fact that Genaro Martín told him, "Go away, Jacinto San José, they may consider you an accomplice and that will cost you dearly," but Jacinto, all the same, returned to his house again and again, always with something to eat, and as soon as he came in the door the little ones would tear the package out of his hands and fight over it on the floor like animals, scratching and biting one another, and Jacinto would place his blue-veined hand commiseratingly on genaro martín's ragged shoulder and try to persuade him, he would say, "Now you see how much good words do, genaro martín, to confuse you and make you say what you didn't say, can you imagine what would happen if the day came when every citizen could talk to three billion other citizens? Listen, genaro martín, the day that the genaromartíns have an intelligible language to ask the DARIOESTEBANS for explanations, the genaromartíns will die because nothing infuriates the DARIOESTEBANS as much as having the genaromartíns ask them for explanations."

Several days later Jacinto San José signed an Intercession Request in the presence of Don Abdón and, after six months had passed, the request was reconsidered and genaromartín's expulsion, owing to the concession of retroactive clemency, was changed to demotion: genaromartín lost his position on the bureaucratic scale and entered the sub-subaltern scale. And the good folk said, "What a big heart this man has!" or, "Don Abdón is the most motherly father of all fathers," or, "If he'd come across me instead of Don Abdón, he'd be singing a different tune," that's what the good folk said.

And the good folk took advantage of the city's annual festival, St. Abdón Martyr, to regale and propitiate Don

Abdón for a whole week, and, for a whole week, the city burst out in celebrations and during them, all those who in the course of the year had showed signs of resistance or noncooperation were subjected to innocent harassments, artless chastisements which ranged from The Invitation to City Hall to The King of Clubs to The Target at the Fair. Actually, new punishments were invented every year, each of them more effective and ingenious than the ones before, but it was those three which particularly aroused popular glee. The first of them, The Invitation to City Hall, consisted of inviting the resister or noncooperator to the main balcony of City Hall so that he could contemplate from that vantage point the fireworks which began or ended the festivities, and once the firework display had begun, the Mayor and members of the Corporation, protected by asbestos clothing and gauntlets and masks, forced the guest against the balustrade so that he would receive in his face the rain of rockets aimed by the crowd, some by hand and some making use of bows and peashooters, right at him. It was a childish game, mere pyrotechnics, in view of the fact that the burns were very rarely as severe as the third degree.

The King of Clubs constituted a pastime which, owing to its aggressiveness and the confusions to which it gave rise, offered greater attraction to the common people. Among the Giants and Bigheads, enormous puppets which circulated through the streets, enlivened by the municipal brass band, and which symbolically attacked the public with balloons and inflated bladders, was hidden one, the King of Clubs, whose cudgel was real and who confined himself to feinting and simulated blows until he encountered the noncooperative or resistant person (who was witnessing the parade from the curb), in which case the King of Clubs delivered the blow on his head after a few friendly threats, in such a way that the person attacked received the stroke with a smile on his lips, believing that it was only a bladder or a balloon, and his misapprehension aroused great hilarity among large and small, who crowded around to see the victim hit the ground. Though occasionally cruel, the game, which local wits called Trepanation, was taken care of even in the worst of cases by a dozen clamps at the Don Abdón Hospital.

Lastly, in The Target at the Fair, the trick was that any citizen with a steady hand, either man or woman, could administer the punishment and, incidentally, win a box of toffee. The technique of the game was rudimentary. Behind the targets, with a hole punched in the center, of the shooting galleries was placed the right eye of the resistant or noncooperative person, suitably restrained by his fellow citizens, in such a way that the presumed victim could watch the aspirants to the prize aiming at his pupil. It was not easy to hit the target, for old, rusty compressed-air guns were used for this purpose and their pressure was very uncertain, but the suspect's nervousness was in itself a side-splitting comic spectacle, and on the other hand, the spectators could cling to the hope that the person firing the gun (almost always by sheer chance) would make a hit, in which case a howl from the noncooperator or resister, usually accompanied by a spectacular fainting fit, would follow the self-advertising cry by the shooting gallery's owner, "Prize for the gentleman!" or "Prize for the young lady!" and when this happened the crowd would gather round and make delighted comments: "Shee-it, that's some eye they gave him!" or: "There's one guy who won't see straight again." In the galleries where this kind of shooting was practiced the conditions were all the same: a box of best-quality toffee for the person who hit the pupil and a yellow package with four pieces of chewing gum if the pellet hit the white of the eye. For obvious reasons, those who were blind in the right eye, those with burns on their faces, and those with a scar on their foreheads were not well regarded in the city.

But the very height of merrymaking took place on the last day of the fair, the feast day of the martyr. As evening fell Don Abdón, attired in a white tunic which left one breast bare and which, creased into innumerable pleats, fell to his feet (shod in gold sandals), would embark, after having been censed, anointed, and crowned with laurel, in the Ship of Destiny. Previously the Don Abdón Electric Company had left the city in darkness and the lake in the woods reflected the thousand lights of the torches and flares and many-colored Japanese lanterns. In the shifting light of the flames, surrounded by the townspeople who silently crowded its banks, Don Abdón's boat would take the three symbolic turns around the little island in the middle along with a dog and a cat shut in a basket and as soon as the circle of the third wake was complete, the townsfolk burst into cheers and ovations as the boat came alongside the dock and six old women belonging to the Little Sisters of Don Abdón, dressed in black and with kerchiefs on their heads that were also black, approached the boat and Susanita Rey Expósito, head of the community, with the weight of her hundred and twenty-three years on her shoulders, went to the steps of the wharf and, after a ceremonious bow, said,

"Descend from your carriage
and receive our homage"

and Don Abdón, disentangling himself from the wreaths of roses and carnations that covered the boat, descended from his floating throne amid the cheers of the multitude and sat, arrogant and affable, upon the interlaced hands of the six old women from the old ladies' home, who, when they received the delicious weight upon themselves, roused by the crowd's thunderous applause, ran and ran like black cockroaches along the paths of the park, with Don Abdón in air, amid a fantastic combination of contrasting lights, singing at the tops of their voices,

"Make a chair, make a chair,
for the queen with golden hair.
Comb it down, comb it down,
see the lice run around."

Beneath the wavering light of the flares and torches, the old women would run, humped and swift, and Don Abdón would laugh and laugh, would totter on his throne, and his white tunic would slip to one side leaving his solid, maternal breasts exposed and, to maintain his superiority and show a proper attitude, he would tightly clutch the bony shoulders of the hundred-year-old women who, when they finished their song, would stop in the center of the Don Abdón Fountain and, bravely ignoring their exhaustion, would stoop down and, bravely ignoring their exhaustion, would shout,

"One, two, three,
upsy-daisy!"

And, simultaneously, they would tense their wasted arms and toss Don Abdón into the air only to catch him again, as he fell, on their trembling interlaced hands and Don Abdón would almost choke with the laughter this caused him and his gusts of laughter spread to the crowd carried away by the spectacle and the laughter of the crowd carried away by the spectacle spread to Don Abdón who made funny noises like nursing babies' when they laugh and would say, would always say, "Do it again, do it again; I like it even better than last year," and the little old ladies, more and more exhausted, would toss him up again, catapulting him to the lowest branches of the chestnut trees in the square, and the excited crowd would demand, "Higher, higher!" and the little old ladies, bravely ignoring their exhaustion, would toss him even higher and the spectators who were in the know would look at each other and remark, "They're doped, otherwise you can't understand how they do it," they would remark, and things went on like this until the hundred-year-olds fell exhausted on the sand of the square and the public cheered their prowess and said "Bravo!" and Don Abdón, as soon as he saw that the little old ladies were incapable of getting up again, would stand up sulkily, tighten his tunic on his left shoulder, ask for his wallet and give a shiny coin to each: "To buy sunflower seeds," he would say paternally and the little old ladies would thank him for the present in their thin, breathless voices, "God bless you," "Health to repeat it next year," they would tell him, and as Don Abdón settled himself in his carriage and the crowd began to disperse, the Don Abdón Electric Company would turn the lights on and they, the little old ladies, would gather under a streetlight, examine and re-examine the coins close up, taking turns biting them with their two decayed teeth, and Rosa San José Expósito would say, "I'm going to order the Samson bodybuilding method for Oldest Sister so she can toss him higher next year; he deserves everything we can give him." And Susanita Rey Expósito would slowly roll up the sleeve of her black dress, bend up her skinny little arm and say ostentatiously, "Just look what a bump," and Encarna Expósito Don Abdón would marvel, "Jeez, look what a bump Susanita just raised!"

When he wakes up his right biceps hurts terribly; he feels as if his arm were dislocated, as if it had a broken spring, and if he stretches it out he can barely make it bend again. He observes that it is as if, overnight, rust had grown in his joints. But it isn't the pain that wakes him (he thinks), rather the gabbling noise, twi-twi-trui-trui-chwick-chwick, of trills, twitterings, and squawks which reach him through the glass of the windows. Jacinto turns over and stretches out on his right side, then on the left, and finally on the right again. It makes no difference. He can't get back to sleep and, in view of this, he gets out of bed, wraps himself in his bathrobe, puts on his bedroom slippers, and goes outside.

The first rays of the sun are dissipating the rime on the mountain slope and silence is slowly beginning to return after the birds' waking twitters. He takes the hose and absent-mindedly screws it onto the tap of the water trough, and as he aims the nozzle at the hedge, observes the progress it has made. It is no longer a timidly sprouted strip but a vegetable mass in which the greenish-white color of the night before has been replaced by the fully developed adult plant and its consequent blossoming. The hedge has grown at least a handsbreadth and the leaves (strong, stiff leaves with sharp edges) set off yellow flowers with delicate stamens, in full bloom. "This is simply unimaginable," Jacinto says to himself, but the sudden entrance of the treecreeper into his field of vision distracts his attention, and when he sees it (the treecreeper) light on one of the logs of the cabin, teet-teet, he (Jacinto) smiles and tells it, "I was afraid you'd gone away," he tells it, but the bird observes him curiously and, without displaying the slightest nervousness, slips, teet-teet, down the log and disappears into a crack. Jacinto waters the strip of hedge and the strip next to it (the one he planted the night before) which so far shows no signs of plant life except that the soil has already started to crack. He waters meticulously (with the same concentration with which he used to write in the office) distributing the water equably, going over the ground he has watered a second time as soon as the little pools that have formed are absorbed. The temperature is quite low, chilly, but the sun, in a cloudless sky, is already making its springtime strength felt. Jacinto sticks his forefinger into the nozzle and achieves a fan of water which falls on the plants in a fine spray, without harming them. Sometimes, because of the way the water emerges and the way the sun's rays catch it, a shimmering rainbow appears in the center of the spray. Jacinto smiles gently and forgets his weakness. After he has taken a turn around the house, he goes to the log gate and opens and shuts it a dozen times. In a mere forty-eight hours the gate has acquired meaning: the hedge already marks out a surface, encloses a space. He (Jacinto) sits on the topmost log of the gate and gently swings back and forth in a pendular movement. Idly, he looks off at a distance, and suddenly sees a hare hopping around on the opposite slope; it (the hare) advances fearlessly and, at intervals, crouches in the clearings, its ears erect, as if waiting for something. Jacinto smiles again, but, all at once, he feels cold and has twinges in his right biceps. He stands up and, before entering the hut, takes in the hedge with a glance and says aloud, "In a week it will be complete. I never saw anything like it."

As he gets into bed he (Jacinto) shivers. He puts on a sweater, spreads his bathrobe on top of the blankets, curls up and pulls the covers over his shoulders. He is beginning to improve. There in bed, he feels better, lying quiet and not talking. Since he said goodbye to Darío Esteban he hasn't missed having company, nor has he even turned on his transistor. "As far as I'm concerned, words are superfluous," he (Jacinto) tells himself.

At first, when Genaro brought up the subject of the

Group, Jacinto thought that indeed the world needed fresh and universal words and that in consequence Esperanto could be a solution and he enrolled in it hoping for great things, but he soon regretted having done so because he realized that when people talk, they argue; when they argue, they hate; and when they hate, they kill. That was when he (Jacinto) said, fewer and newer words. Genaro observed him deep in thought (he frequently surprised him sitting on a chair, rubbing his head, or meditating alone on the tops of the hills around the city) and a few weeks later Jacinto set forth for the first time the objective of his movement THROUGH SILENCE TO PEACE. (It was something still incipient, not yet formed, but with a promising appearance and undoubted inner strength.) Jacinto said, "We threw away our chance with the Tower of Babel but, though it's late, there's still time." To tell the truth, very few people listened to him (Jacinto) and most of that minority made fun of him; Darío Esteban himself, who heard him holding forth one morning in the Refectory, said to him, "Don't talk foolishness, Jacinto San José; you'd better talk about the 3-3-4. Do you think that the 3-3-4 is an effective offensive tactic or, on the other hand, a sensible defensive strategy?" and Jacinto wrinkled his nose in a sort of smile and said, "Sorry, I don't indulge," to which Darío Esteban replied, waggling his neck from side to side like a chicken on the alert, "Are you questioning the fact, Jacinto San José, that talking about sports is even healthier than practicing them?"

After this dissident observation Jacinto decided to speak using only the strictly necessary words. The conversations in the Refectory and when going in and out of the office struck him as a senseless waste, and only when he chatted with the mirror did he allow himself a bit of license, owing to the fact that he (Jacinto) could at most destroy his reflection (the mirror), but such an act of aggression was not serious in itself nor would it bring unpleasant consequences for anyone. Convinced of the good sense of his idea, he set himself, over the course of several days, to find disciples. The first would-be adherent was César Fuentes (nicknamed Cesarina) who, no sooner had Jacinto opened his mouth, stated his radical disagreement: You'd have to cut the tongue off all rational beings (what César Fuentes said, in his high-pitched little voice, was "castrate their mouths") to smother verbal acts of aggression in embryo. Jacinto tried to have a heart-to-heart talk with him and told him, "Be careful, César Fuentes, theories born out of resentment have very little chance of succeeding and if they did succeed they would generate nothing but resentment; if trying to understand one another is utopian, there's only one possibility for understanding: not to try."

Apart from César Fuentes, two men attracted Jacinto from the first, for obvious reasons: Baudelio Villamayor the gardener, because of his laconic speech, and the Class I clerk Eutilio Crespo because of his instinct for hiding things. Baudelio Villamayor, ever since he entered the Company, had made himself understood with half sentences or half words, so that when he said "Morning" it was perfectly obvious that he meant "Good morning," and if he said "Good" it was perfectly obvious that he meant "Good afternoon," and, insofar as Eutilio Crespo was concerned, Jacinto observed that he was so zealous a guardian of his personality that he usually hid what he was writing behind a cardboard fan to keep from being plagiarized. Both Baudelio Villamayor and Eutilio Crespo accepted the guidelines of the movement THROUGH SILENCE TO PEACE and, except for them, Jacinto's words fell on deaf ears. This did not keep Jacinto from continuing to develop his theories, seeking the bases of his doctrine, and one afternoon when he expressed his motto: "Neither rhetoric nor dialectic; short sentence, short word, long thought," Baudelio Villamayor objected that he could handle the short sentence and the short word all right, but how the fuck was he going to manage to have a long thought. This objection offered new reasons for reflection on Jacinto's part, and finally he summed up his thought in the following conclusions:

a) It is not rational that all of man's strength should slip away from him through his mouth. b) The spoken word, up to now, has scarcely served for anything but an instrument of aggression or a display of foolishness. c) Words are used to construct paradises inaccessible to the legs, and d) and lastly, the fewer words we pronounce and the shorter they are, fewer and shorter will be the acts of aggressiveness and stupidity that float around the world.

The part about long thought was, therefore, set aside for the moment. And so, without Jacinto's really meaning to invent it, contracto was born.

Chopped-off words, especially multisyllabic ones, gained in euphony and, in the context of the sentence, became perfectly intelligible; they saved time not only for the speaker and writer but also for those who heard or read them; when the dictionary was restated, the new words recovered the initial energy and purity of which use and abuse (erosion, according to Jacinto) had deprived them; the risk of verbal automatism, a direct cause of floating stupidity, was avoided, and lastly, the probabilities of discord were lessened because he who talks a lot errs a lot and he who talks little, errs little.

César Fuentes, Baudelio Villamayor, and Eutilio Crespo smiled as they gave him the approving pat on the back (the traditional ovation had been reduced, in contracto, to a single pat, since this action expressed both assent and pleasure, without wasting time or uselessly burning up energy). Jacinto performed the first demonstration with the now-famous slogan: "Neither rhetoric nor dialectic; every attempt at comprehension through the spoken word is a utopia," which, in contracto, was reduced to this: "Neithe rheto nor diale; eve attem at comprensa through the spowo is a uto." César Fuentes, Baudelio Villamayor, and Eutilio Crespo gave him another pat and César Fuentes said "Marve!" and Eutilio Crespo said "Wonderf!" and Baudo Villamo, the garde, looked first to one side and then the other, conscious of the fact that he was participating in the start of something important but without entirely taking in its transcendent importance. (In the course of time, Jacinto would come to recognize the influence of his innate aversion to multisyllabic words in the genesis of contracto. His timidity prevented him from speaking a multisyllabic word without an incipient stammer, almost a stutter, and this made his discomfort all the greater. Thanks to contracto these words were now shortened, and multisyllabic words became soothing without being overwhelming.)

Jacinto spent hours and hours perfecting and polishing the new language. He often said to himself with secret pleasure, "Contracto is me," and this phrase, while it soothed his tiny sense of vanity, also inspired him with a feeling of responsible nervousness. He had faith in its universal acceptance; fewer and shorter words might be the regulating element needed by humanity and, convinced of this, Jacinto set for the Eve of St. Joseph (perhaps a bit precipitately) the Init Congre of Contro.

The meeting was held in Baudelio Villamayor's greenhouse among the potted plants, spades, and rakes, around a charcoal brazier and a few glasses of red wine. Jacinto's discourse, a model of verbal economy, was taken down in its entirety by Eutilio Crespo in the Recording Secretary's book where, after the initial meeting, not another word was ever written. It ran as follows:

(Comple text of disco of Move through Silen to Peace pronoun by Don Jazo San José Niño.)

"Belov associas: a few syllabs to give you welco and tell you that we are making progre. It is a necessi for Humani to save syllabs. It is very dange to talk more than we think. Also, an exce of syllabs leads to confusa. It is an erro to think that a univ langua would help us live toge. Rheto, grandiloque, interfe with huma comprehensa. Let us be laco and try to cause humas to talk as little as possi with other humas, for if one huma speaks less with ano huma, disagre is impossi and therefo we will reach a defini perio of harmo. Think of the tremen importa of this histo momen. That is all. Let us elect a Presi, a Vicepresi, a Secre, a Vicesecre, and a Treasu to do the work of our associata."

A single dry, unanimous clapping sound was heard, like a lid snapping shut, but when the time came to elect officers it was found necessary to leave the office of Vicesecre vacant owing to lack of numbers. After his election as Presi, Jacinto had to be everywhere at once to take care of consultations, avoid friction, and solve difficult situations, but, despite his zealous efforts, a conflict appeared in the section on Demands and Questas. "Endings in -tion and -sion contract to ta or sa by simple eupho," said Jacinto. "Exa: precaution becomes precauta and confusion becomes confusa." "Verb tenses, except for the past parti, do not contract. Exa: slep for slept, comprehed for comprehended." "Bisyllabs, genera speaking, do not contract. Exceptas: proper names and those ending in consonas. Exa: Ceso Fuenta and erro for error."

Eutilio Crespo, with his proverbial mistrustfulness, interrupted Jacinto every little while, demanding explanations as if he (Jacinto) were trying to cheat them, and eventually began to accuse him of wanting to do everything himself, so rudely that little by little the friendly dialogue degenerated into a bitter polemic. First Eutilio Crespo said, "If verb tenses don't contra with the excepta of the past parti, we produ no progre, Jazo." Second, Jacinto replied, "But think, Euto, that we're trying to make a differ but understanda langua." Third, seeing that things were taking an awkward turn and meaning to avoid a leadership crisis, César Fuentes chimed in, "One momen, I'm going to read the first translata into contro of a sonne by Anto Macho," but Eutilio Crespo (fourth) interpreted César Fuentes' intervention as a provocation and got angry and yelled, "None of your tomfoo, now! The proble is more serio than all that," and, as Jacinto, though he tried to calm them down, waving his blue-veined hands, did not budge an inch (fifth), Eutilio Crespo lost his head (sixth) and yelled at him, "You're a dicto and a nincomp!" he told him, and although Jacinto feebly drew attention to his position as Presi of the newly established association, Eutilio Crespo, beside himself (seventh), knocked the bench over backward, stood up and, at the top of his voice, closed off any possibility of agreement: "So the Presi can kiss my assho!" he screamed, and total confusion ensued and, as Jacinto was saying, "One momen, please," César Fuentes insisted on reading the sonne of Anto Macho and Baudelio Villamayor, the gardener, grabbed Eutilio Crespo by his lapels and shook him violently and called him "basta" and "knowita" and Eutilio Crespo, after escaping from his grip (eighth and lastly), seized the doorknob and told him, "Go fuck yourself, you shitty garde," he told him, and slammed the door as he went out.

The doctor gives him no respite:

A silence ensued which Jacinto broke by saying dejectedly, "It's been a failu, I'm sorry. Us humas are just hopele." And Baudelio Villamayor, his eyes on the ground, waved them (or shoved them) toward the door, go on, beat it, just our luck if the Boss comes by; and they left, and as they walked on the cinder paths in the starlight, César Fuentes took Jacinto San José by the arm and told him sadly. "That sonofa, Euto, is always so stubbo, and the worst of it is that he's too stupi to come in out of the rain."

87

The doctor takes a little celluloid ball and an egg made of the same material, both white, out of his desk drawer, blinks, and holds up one in each hand.

"One moment," he says. "Quick, grasp the egg."

Jacinto stretches out his hand and grasps the egg.

"Now," says the doctor, "take the other egg."

Jacinto again smiles meekly, as if realizing that he has been made the butt of a joke, and, meekly, says, "I'm sorry, doctor, there are no more eggs. What's left is a ball, not an egg."

The doctor gives him no respite:

"Tell me, is your head an egg or a ball?"

Jacinto clears his throat.

"It's neither an egg nor a ball," he answers firmly, "it's a head, but if we really must look for resemblances, its shape is a little more like an egg than a ball."

The doctor wrinkles his brow and his keen gaze becomes somber. He then raises the little white sphere above his shoulder and asks, "And if I were to tell you that this is a zero, what would you answer?"

Jacinto squints visibly out of his left eye and, to calm himself, sticks his hand between two of his shirt buttons and clutches his golden medal. He says, "I would say that it isn't a zero, it's a ball."

"That's strange. And what's the difference between them?"

"Well," says Jacinto, "so we'll understand each other I will say that the zero is something that can't be grasped, it doesn't exist, it's just a drawing."

The doctor's eyes and brow grow even more somber. Now he murmurs insistently under his breath, "Golly,

88

golly, golly," and writes without interruption on the back of the file card but, suddenly, stops and says (to Jacinto) without looking at him, "I'm sure that this trouble of yours is nothing but a garden-variety adding neurosis. Tomorrow I'll send the diagnosis and treatment to the main office."

Jacinto waits patiently in an at-ease position, and just as the doctor opens the door and tells him "Go along," he goes out, but immediately, when he is still on the threshold, the doctor's hand catches his arm in a viselike grip and Jacinto turns around and sees the white egg between the doctor's swarthy fingers and hears his voice:

"Excuse me; is this object I have in my hand a zero or an O?"

Jacinto lets slip a sly giggle, like a peasant's.

"It's neither one nor the other," he says. "It's an egg."

Without apparent justification, the doctor begins to fire questions at him point-blank, without giving him (Jacinto) time to recover from the previous one (the question). He (the doctor) points with his ballpoint pen to the zero of April 10 on the calendar that hangs from a hook in the corridor.

"And this?" he (the doctor) adds. "Is it a ball or an egg?"

"It's a zero," answers Jacinto.

"And here? Do you mind telling me what it says here?" He points to the capital O of the month of October.

Jacinto hesitates for a moment.

"It says O," he says at last.

"It's not a zero? Look carefully ! This is important."

"No, doctor, it's an O, I'm sure."

"And what makes you so sure that it's an O and not a zero?"

Jacinto is no longer laughing; he feels that he is dripping with sweat and observes that there is a sort of film before his eyes which deforms the objects he sees.

"Eh? Answer!"

"Otherwise," says Jacinto submissively, "it would say 'Ctober.' A zero there would make no sense, doctor, you must understand that."

"No, right? but notice something, this isn't a question of meaning but of typography. Take that thing you call an O and put it back here (he points to the zero of April 10), then what would happen?"

Jacinto cocks his head on one side in confusion.

"What would happen," he says in a thin little voice, stammering, "is that it would be 100 instead of 10."

"But didn't we agree that this was an O?"

"Let's see if I can explain myself, doctor; among letters it's an O; among numbers it would be a zero."

"That's ridiculous! Are you trying to tell me that in your handwriting the zero and the O have nothing to differentiate them? Do you mind telling me what it says here?" (he continues to point to April 10).

"Ten," says Jacinto.

"Concentrate, please; don't answer off the top of your head. Are you sure that it doesn't say LO?"

"Absolutely sure, doctor."

"That's good. And why does it have to be that way?"

"Those are numbers, doctor. It would be absurd if it said eight, nine, L0, eleven . . . don't you understand?

Excuse me, but I don't know how to explain it any other way."

Before Jacinto has finished speaking, the doctor places the ballpoint upright beside the celluloid ball.

"And here? What does it say here? Ten or L0?"

Jacinto passes the back of his hand over his forehead, which is dripping with sweat. He tries to get control of himself and answers, "That doesn't say anything, doctor. That's a ballpoint next to a ball."

"A ball, you say? Sure? It wouldn't be, by any chance, an egg? Concentrate!"

When he opens his eyes, the first thing that he (Jacinto) sees in the fog is the doctor's piercing and troubled eyes, but they (his eyes) are white and bulging as if he had the two celluloid balls set into the sockets. And his (the doctor's) lips form grimaces and make little noises as if he were talking (or swearing) to himself.

"Do you feel better?" The doctor's voice has the rise and fall of distant thunder.

Jacinto makes a move to sit up.

"Wait a minute, there's no hurry," adds the doctor in a more humane voice. "I presume that I owe you an explanation. Our profession is a difficult one, believe me, but this test was unavoidable. The patient, by instinct, barricades himself behind what he believes to be his personality, but this may not exist, it may be a mere potentiality. The patient, however, tries not to admit it because he is by definition a vain, stubborn, and impervious being. To make him relax and to obtain a spontaneous reaction from him, we must previously have emptied him, depersonalized him. You do understand me, don't you?"

Jacinto is still lying face up, too weak to move. The mere fact of opening his eyes tires him and gives him a painful numbness in the frontal sinuses (Don Abdón's turgid breasts might, perhaps, give him back the old sensation of lost security.) But he does open them (his eyes) and, as he does so (opens his eyes), he sees, parallel to his body, the tigerwood boards that cover the room's ceiling and begins to count them one by one, paying special attention to the arrangement of the grooves between them and to the grain and knots in each board so as not to make a mistake. When he has finished, he starts over. From the wall to the bookcase which separates the bedroom from the living room, there are thirty-three boards, stained walnut-color. But something extraordinary happens to him (Jacinto): as he passes (mentally) the tens (10, 20, 30) the nausea comes again, spasmodically and very strongly. "Now I can't even think about zero," Jacinto tells himself, frightened. The cawing of a rook nearby, kaa, seems to pierce him like a dagger, and to exorcise his fears and anxiety he mechanically fondles the medal on his breast (the swollen breasts of Don Abdón might offer a refuge for his fearfulness). Jacinto begins to pray; he prays under his breath but with great devotion until he is distracted by the cold in his feet, a deep mineral cold which resists both blankets and rubbing. He tries to get up but the mere idea of doing so (of trying, not getting up) leaves him exhausted. He sticks one hand out of the covers and, without moving the rest of his body, suddenly tugs on the cord of the

Venetian blind, ra-ta-bla, and the light suddenly comes in through the displaced slats. The light makes him (Jacinto) feel better, you could say that he breathes better, as if it were air instead of light that was coming in through the windowpanes. Without realizing it, he is adding up the boards in the ceiling again and, all of a sudden, his eyes begin to bulge and he screams: "Am I going to die here like a dog?" he yells, and as he says this his gaze slides from board to board, slips past the shelves of the bookcase and finally rests on the melancholy antelope's head on the chimneypiece, and as he encounters its empty glass stare Jacinto's blue-veined hands clench on the bedspread.

Jacinto is neither particularly stupid nor particularly smart but he is sufficiently so (smart, that is) to try to defend his limited intelligence. To do this (defend it) he knows that he must appeal to personal choice and not delegate it. And if Don Abdón pays him for two meals a day, a soccer match every two weeks, and the monthly installment on the television set, and Darío Esteban says that to give less is exploitation and to give more a subtle form of corruption, all right, even if they tell him that (Don Abdón and Darío Esteban), he (Jacinto) goes and makes his choice and tells himself: No television set, no soccer; two books a month, a loaf of bread for the birds in the park and a begonia, a sansevieria, and a ficus in my room. And he still had something left over to buy Doña Palmira, if she caught the grippe, half a dozen red carnations to make her convalescence pleasanter. This was what Jacinto did and though he was not dissatisfied with himself, sometimes he felt afraid because the words of his officemates and those of the newspapers seemed more cryptic every day, despite the fact that they (his officemates) seemed to get very excited and even proud of their conversations and he (Jacinto) would be happy if he could manage to share this passion just once in his life, but it was not viable for him (to share this passion) because the fervor of his officemates came from sources that were closed to him: the catenaccio defense, Perry Mason, midfielder, The Invaders, and negative points in soccer. And so Jacinto gradually felt more and more alien to the world around him, as isolated as if he were in a desert, and he would say to himself, "The Tower of Babel was our only chance," Jacinto would say to himself firmly, and he thought that a glance or a facial expression possessed greater possibilities of expression and constituted a more sincere vehicle of communication than a torrent of words, for words had become hermetic, ambiguous, or empty by losing their virginity.

Jacinto fears lack of communication because Jacinto, like every thinking man, is faint-hearted, and the afternoon that Eutilio Crespo suddenly turned on him and said, "So the Presi can kiss my assho," he (Jacinto) felt intuitively that the last door of the labyrinth had closed upon him and that night, when he got home, he wept over the begonia, the sansevieria, and the ficus imagining that by watering them with his tears they were definitely his and would understand him better. (That is, what Jacinto seeks and never finds is something stable to hang on to, a swelling breast or a plant, to cling to in order to survive.)

Another of Jacinto's fears is his limitedness. One day

he performs a self-examination and reaches the bitter conclusion that he only knows how to do four things: read books about the sea, add, crumble bread, and water plants. Physiological functions apart, Jacinto doesn't know how to do anything else. He doesn't know, for example, how to subtract, multiply, or divide, nor does he know, for example, how to put together sentences whose last words rhyme to make a verse. He has an idea, of course, that "June" and "moon" rhyme but he does not know how many and what words he has to place before those two to make them match. Don Abdón, in his annual speeches, reminds them that unilateral education, specialization, frees men from emotional servitude. Jacinto doesn't understand this very well, he doesn't understand it at all, but he accepts it (accepts his specialization) because, though it seems paradoxical, submitting to it (to specialization) is the only chance to get closer to the emotional servitude of Don Abdón's suffocating udders (though this unhealthy proclivity worries Jacinto a great deal), in which he vaguely senses the security of long ago.

Don Abdón's reasoning is logical, or seems to be, but the appalling thing is that logic has also begun to terrify Jacinto, because the day that Don Abdón said, "Progress depends on practical things and knowledge on knowing how to add," he acted in consistency with his words and had the cedars cut down, the cedars, tall and leafy as cathedrals, which had shaded the building for half a century, and had had hedges planted in their stead (the hedge is the defense of the timid), hedges of box, climbing roses, borders of geraniums, and cinder paths and, at the same time, had given orders to change the pictures representing landscapes, bucolic and local-color scenes and old-fashioned engravings for diagrams, ornithograms, and mathematical symbols. It was on that very day that Jacinto bought the begonia, the sansevieria, and the ficus to give himself something to rest his eyes on and to relax in vegetal harmony when he returned from the office.

Jacinto also fears the redeemers who redeem with the same rod they use to strike, those who see the mote in the eye of others and not the beam in their own, crowds, and games involving large numbers of spectators. Hence, though Amando García urges him to accompany him as a spectator to an Invitation to City Hall, to a King of Clubs, or a Target at the Fair, even admitting that they are decadent pastimes and a bit vulgar, he (Jacinto) refuses because seeing a scorched face, a head laid open by a blow from a club, or an eye put out by bird shot are scenes which still do not please him and although the others laugh and he (Jacinto) tries to overcome his morbid hypersensitivity, he simply can't help it: he suffers. He accepts the fact that some times give way to other times and even recognizes regression, for if there is nothing new under the sun, men must necessarily regress and keep going round and round in their tracks like donkeys drawing water from a well, pretending that they are advancing and refusing to recognize that they have arrived. He (Jacinto) even accepts revolutionism (though he would be repelled by a son like Genaro) but it depresses him and, then, it turns out that if he (Jacinto) does not believe in words as communication, he does not know his officemates' language, he fears re-deemers, he is pained by regression, he is depressed by revolutionism, he gets dizzy when he writes zeroes, it scares him to have Eutilio Crespo tell him, "So the Presi can kiss my assho," and he needs a pair of opulent breasts to nestle against, then it turns out that it is life which frightens him (Jacinto), but since death also frightens him, he (Jacinto) finds himself in a blind alley and when he cries out, staring fixedly at the antelope's tormented glass eyes, "Am I going to die here like a dog?", when he cries that, in the depths of his despair, he is sure that someone will hear him, will have pity on him, will take him in his or her arms, will rock him, will press him against his or her breast and squeeze out of his body, first in spurts and then drop by drop (like a wet sheet when it is wrung), all the fear he has inside. But nobody hears him, nobody has pity on him, nobody picks him up because in the ravine, and, it seems, in the uplands, for a hundred kilometers around, there is no one. And by spells (perhaps hours) Jacinto dozes and, when he wakes, mechanically adds up the boards in the ceiling and, between one nap and another, hears the cooing of a turtle dove, roo-coo, or the cawing of a rook, kaa, or the whistle of a blackbird, tsee, or the cry of a jay, chack-chack, or (when the striped light from the blind has lessened) the nightingale's iterative concert, chook-chook-piu-piu-piu, or the slightly lugubrious call of an owl from the top of the elm tree, kiu, or the clucking sound of a nightjar, goo-ek, which, as is its custom, is hunting mosquitoes on the road.

Despite his lack of appetite, his extreme weakness, he

(Jacinto) understands, in a flash of lucidity, that he cannot live without eating and instinctively flings himself out of bed, hastens to the kitchen on tiptoe and returns (also on tiptoe) to bed with some boiled ham, half a cheese, a chunk of bread, and a bottle of red wine, and slips it all under the blankets (while he pants from the exertion), holds it close to his body to warm it with his fever because, according to Doña Palmira, cold foods are the ones that harm the stomach and cause ulcers and, after a few minutes have passed, he sits up and eats (biting into the ham and the cheese, without cutting them) and gulps straight out of the bottle and feels chills running up and down his back, like slugs. When he has finished he makes a new effort, jumps out of bed and shuts himself in the toilet (gentlemen) but, since he is alone in the world, he doesn't shoot the bolt ("prejudices of a petit-bourgeois period," says Amando García) and urinates quietly, without nervousness, enjoying the sight of the liquid parabola, transparent even though it (the urine) is heavy with fever. Without meaning to, he (Jacinto) catches sight of himself in the mirror, and he says hello and tells himself, *Jacinto, for heaven's sake, man, what are you doing here? you sure have great luck, you're not good for a thing, my boy, whoever would think of getting sick now? Of course maybe it's the neurosis itself that's giving you the fever, it's anybody's guess, the Doctor couldn't have been less explicit, eat well, sleep well, get out in the fresh air and these pills, very simple, but in what apothecary's shop can you buy a good appetite and sleep? That's what I say, Jacinto, though, after all, others are worse off, it's not that I'm complaining, understand, it's only that I don't* have anybody to call on, that's the only thing, you know that, as for the rest, patience, now when this is over, Jacinto, you're going to pass the buck, d'you hear? don't go back on me, you'll pass the buck and that's all there is to it, like the others, naturally, what a guy can't do he can't do, it's a great luxury to want to swim against the current, I'll say, losing an eye isn't exactly nothing, you'll pass the buck and that's all. Ha! that's right, now you're laughing, that's all you needed, Jacinto, but are you in your right mind? you're really in a fine pickle, more alone you couldn't be, my boy, like a leper, exactly like that, the first thing is to learn your officemates' language, d'you hear? and then don't go off on tangents, catenaccio, midfielder, The Invaders, and all that; I don't think it's so hard, all you need is a little bit of nerve and to stop being foolish, because after all just because you speak their language doesn't mean that floating stupidity is going to increase all that much in the world, Jacinto, and if it does increase, well, let it increase, what simply can't be is for you to have a head like yours at your age, my boy, whiter than your grandmother's, if you told anybody how old you are he'd never believe it, honest to God! and if it's true that every idea gives you a white hair, then don't have ideas, my fine friend, nobody makes you have them, remember Genaro, Jacinto, don't tell me, like a beggar, from door to door, and not even a crust, I mean not a crust, naturally, after all if a man is knocking himself out to think for you and keep you from having responsibilities and then you come along, with your pretty face, and pay him back by asking questions, then you're ungrateful, that's right, don't be a dog in the manger, don't turn it over and over, but they did turn him around and around, and "Once more, once

99

more!'' demanded Ginés Gil and Ernesto Blanco (and everybody), carried away, and Amando García, who was watching them with mocking eyes, wiggling his ears, grabbed Jacinto by the shoulders again and twirled him round and round, at high speed, like a top, counter to the earth's rotation, while the others made room for him and nearly died laughing and Amando García, acting drunk, kept repeating, "Listen, this dumbbell gets dizzy when he writes zeroes. Did you ever hear anything like it?" And more and more office clerks kept coming and they kept on laughing and egging Jacinto on, "Faster, faster, faster!" and then they clapped, as if he were dancing for the fun of it, until Jacinto tripped and fell in a sitting position, saliva running from his mouth, onto the cinders of the path and Amando García wiggled his ears as hard as he could to make his predicament more comic and asked, "And now? What do you feel now, Jacinto San José?" and Jacinto blinked and his innocuous, innocent blue eyes seemed strangely darkened, but he closed them and even tried to smile as he answered, "I got dizzy this time too, I admit it," and then Amando García grabbed him by the lapels, made him stand up and spun him again and again amid the laughter of his officemates and the whites of Jacinto's eyes showed, his eyes rolled wildly, and he saw the ground above him and the sky below, and noticed that something was clutching at him down there, in the middle of his belly, or perhaps his stomach, he noticed it, and suddenly, without knowing how or why, he fell face down on the grass and heaved suddenly and he vomited and then came another heave and he vomited again and went on vomiting like this over and over and although he was aware of the wetness of the vomit on his cheek he was unable to move and furthermore his side hurt (because of the spasms) and, fleetingly, he thought that he was throwing up his guts (actually, the curds of his vomit) because the nausea didn't stop and he had nothing left to throw up, but the nausea persisted, it went on for so long that his officemates eventually went away in disappointment, "That's all there is to see," they said, so that Jacinto was left alone in the garden and, after a while, he sat up and saw Gen comma two meters away comma lapping up the stuff that he had just thrown up and comma revolted comma he said, "You simply mustn't do that, Gen, filthy!" comma but Gen comma indifferent to his admonition comma kept gobbling it up and he comma almost helpless comma "Gen, Gen, come here!" comma helpless comma because the sugar-beet plants were clutching at his feet like hands comma but Gen didn't even listen to him comma he jumped over the fence running after the boy who was zigzagging between the furrows to escape his persecution comma terrified comma and the farmer said angrily from a second-story window, "Hey you, get out, mother-fucker!" but Gen comma maddened comma paid no attention and Jacinto and Genaro's twins ran through the alfalfa field comma falling and getting up again comma "Come here!" they screamed comma and when they reached the fig tree that grew near the farmhouse comma the boy grabbed a branch and made an agile leap but Gen comma who seemed entranced by his behind comma braked simultaneously resting his two hands on the ground comma swiveled his head around and intercepted him as he came out from behind the tree and though his first attempt was unsuccessful comma on the second try he caught the right buttock between his teeth comma while Jacinto and the twins were running laboriously now among the stubble rows and the boy was blubbering and the farmer appeared in the doorway with an old double-barreled shotgun and however much Jacinto wanted to say no comma stop comma not to do anything foolish comma that he would take responsibility comma his exhausted breathing haaa-haaa prevented him and all he could do was make urgent gestures with his hands comma but the farmer said now I'm going to get you and without aiming or anything comma holding the gun under his armpit comma he fired two shots at point-blank range comma the second of which almost lifted Gen off the ground comma right up in the air comma and before Gen fell back again under the fig tree comma Jacinto could see the blood already bubbling out of his side and the farmer loaded the shotgun again and turned toward Jacinto who had just come running up comma while the youngster took refuge in the arms of his mother who had come out of the stable at the sound of the detonations with a pail in each hand period Jacinto comma without giving a thought to the weapon comma knelt beside Gen comma placed his right hand on his ribs and rubbed vigorously comma but when he noticed the stertor and convulsions comma he lifted Gen's head and placed his mouth over Gen's and blew whoooo and sucked in wheeee comma blew whoooo and sucked in wheeee comma blew whoooo and sucked in wheeee but the air escaped through the

102

corners of Gen's mouth fssss comma a mouth so long that Jacinto couldn't get it all between his lips comma and he felt desperate because it gave him the sensation of a pump that couldn't be fastened tight to the valve and one of the times that he sucked in wheeee his mouth filled with blood comma thick and sweet comma so much blood that he thought he had sucked Gen dry and the twins who arrived breathless at that very moment comma threw themselves on the outstretched body crying and saying daddy, daddy! and Jacinto stood up spitting and cleaning his mouth with his handkerchief and said you killed him and the farmer agreed and said comma I sure did and who cares? and comma right after that comma he said pointing at the children comma what I won't put up with is people making a fool of me. Do you have the dog tag? and Jacinto wrinkled his brow comma you must mean his identity card comma he said comma and the farmer rested the butt of the shotgun on the ground and leaned on the barrels and said I mean what I said, the dog tag comma he said comma and Jacinto opened his wallet comma searched among the papers and at last held out to the farmer genaromartín's identity card and the farmer looked at it on one side and then the other comma on one side and then the other comma several times and then he said well, I suppose that this guy is the owner comma no it's him comma said Jacinto comma but before he had finished speaking comma the farmer grabbed him by the lapels and lifted him up so far that the tips of his shoes barely touched the ground and told him comma the farmer comma listen here comma the farmer told him comma if after hurting my kid you still think you can laugh in my face you're very much mistaken. Come on, the vaccination certificate, period Jacinto as soon as the farmer released him knelt beside Gen and tried to find the scar of the vaccination on his upper arm by parting the spotted hair but he couldn't find it and murmured nervously by way of justification comma it must be here, but he's grown so much hair . . . and comma after his fruitless search comma he lifted his pale face and said humbly colon in any case I can answer for him; he's an officemate of mine comma but comma unexpectedly comma the farmer lost patience comma grabbed the shotgun and aimed it at Jacinto comma and Jacinto and the twins started back in terror and the farmer said "So he was your officemate, huh? Get out of here! And if you want to see this heap of garbage again you know where to look, tomorrow in the Don Abdón Institute."

Jacinto opens his eyes and for the first time in several days does not feel the blood beating in his temples, twinges in his back, or stabbing pains in the nape of his neck. As he sits up in bed he hears over and over the modulated song of a nightingale, chook-piu-piu-piu, very close to the window. Jacinto smiles to himself: "I'm fine, it's all over," he tells himself. And while he is dressing he tries to whistle, wheee, but his lips have been inactive for so long that they lack elasticity and are as dry and stiff as cardboard. A faint light that allows him to make out the outlines of the furniture is filtering through the slats of the blind. As he puts on his woollen socks he (Jacinto) is assailed by shortness of breath and in view of this he puts his shoes on by stepping on the backs of the heels and leaving them unfastened. As he starts to walk, the first thing that occurs to him is that each of his heavy brogues weighs a ton. But all his exhaustion and weakness melt away when he opens the door of the cabin and comes up against the wall of foliage that cuts off visibility on every side. All of a sudden the sun's rays shine in his eyes and dazzle him so much that he has to stop and protect them (his eyes) with his hand. Little by little he opens his fingers (as slowly as the slats of the blind when he pulls the cord) so that his pupils can get accustomed to the light. While he is waiting for this he can hear the constant splashing of the brook, slap-slap, mingled with the call of a cock partridge, chuck-chuck-er, and the tuneful stridency of the nightingale, chook-piu-piu-piu, behind the hut, probably in the elm trees. But when he opens his eyes he can see neither the brook, nor the cock partridge, nor the mill with the abandoned millstones because the hedge, which is now as tall as his (Jacinto's) eyebrows, gets in the way. His first reaction is childish: "It needs cutting," he (Jacinto) says to himself, but he is aware that what he is trying to do by speaking those words is to dissipate the faint sensation of nervousness that is beginning to gnaw at him, that is, to deceive himself. He steps up to the hedge with his hands in his pockets and thinks, "This is too much," but says aloud, "How beautiful! The day that the earth can be made to produce like this, hunger will disappear from the world." Jacinto is reluctant to confront reality, but he observes that the flexible original stems have divided two, four, eight, sixteen times, that they are joining, entangling, intertwining with one another, and don't let in a single ray of light. In addition, their development is so

105

vigorous that the stems at their base are already as thick as his (Jacinto's) forearm. Generally speaking, the hedge's offshoots are rapidly growing upward in a sort of Gothic verticality, but the progress of the minor branches and tendrils is also remarkable. In this sense its propagation is very industrious. All of Jacinto's botanical interest, which is very great, is now concentrated on the slender creeping branches. The leaf buds give birth to dozens of little shoots like runners, whose widely separated buds take solid root among the cracks in the paving blocks. From them (the buds) other leaf buds sprout and in their turn put out long runners, so that it can even be said that the hedge is moving, that is, walking. And the most frightening thing is that the skin which clothes stems and branches bristles with tiny, extraordinarily tenacious growths like fingernails which, with no posts or walls to cling to, tangle among themselves in an inextricable skein. And among the stiff, notched leaves open short-lived yellow flowers, for the haughty fragrance of some of them contrasts with the wilting of others and the death in tatters of a few. Jacinto continues to watch: in his immobility, he is as if turned to stone. Suddenly he spins around and walks slowly forward, step by step, along the strip of open space between the vegetation and the cabin. His shadow, falling on the paving blocks, precedes him, and as he walks the blackbirds, finches, robins, wrens, and redwings flutter, whirr-whirr, in the thick tangled growth. Jacinto pays no attention to the birds; he is hypnotized by his shadow, and when he sees that it (the shadow of his shoulders) barely fits into the width of the passageway he gives a start, takes his hands

out of his pockets and walks quickly toward the gate
made of pine logs, but as he reaches the corner without
finding it, he turns back and murmurs, "But it was here;
it was right here." His (Jacinto's) nervousness is apparent in the impatience of his movements. He opens the
hedge by separating the branches with both hands and
in his haste grazes his forehead and scratches his left eye.
"Calm down, Jacinto," he says to himself, pressing his
handkerchief to his injured eye, but his actions do not
match his desires. He continues to search, and at length,
among the foliage, he sees the gate half a meter away,
but he (Jacinto) imagines that it is the eye covered by
the handkerchief (which does not stop weeping) that is
producing this deceptive sensation of depth and he un-
covers it, but then he discovers that it is not a half but a
whole meter that separates him from the gate. "Holy Virgin!" he says to himself. Behind it (the gate) he can see
no light either, from which he deduces that the strip he
sowed later has also sprouted. "This is at least four meters thick," he tells himself with logical precision and
opening his eyes very wide (the left eye still bloodshot
and shedding tears) and clenching his fists until his nails
dig into his palms. He hears the noise of his own heart,
tick-tack, tick-tack, jumping inside his chest as he
straightens up, and then he does what birds do when
they are placed in a new cage: he takes several turns
around his prison to make sure that there is not a single
open space, and also that, as far as Jacinto can tell, its
uniformity of growth is another of the American hybrid's characteristics. The thicket is closing him in with
its insidious progress and, in view of this, Jacinto tells

himself, "Calmly now, calmly," takes a deep breath through his nose and exhales it through his mouth in intermittent gusts, pssst-pssst, while he heads for the toolshed, back-to-back with the shed for the water pump. In any case, his appeals to calmness and coolheadedness do him (Jacinto) very little good, for as he opens the door of the shed he catches his right index finger in it, but the pain (which he tries to counteract by putting the finger in his mouth) disappears when he sees the tools that are lined up inside: a hoe, an adze, a sickle, a billhook, an axe, a shovel, a rake, a handsaw, and some pruning shears. Jacinto smiles broadly, like a besieged general who hears the bugles of his reinforcements and, still without taking the finger out of his mouth, uses his other hand to pick up the shears, the saw, the axe, and the adze (which he secures under one arm) and returns to the place where the gate is. As he cuts the stems that are growing out of the hedge, crick-crack, he has a triumphant sensation of power. The shears are heavy and well sharpened. He (Jacinto) catches the smaller branches between their (the shears') powerful jaws, exercises a slight pressure, hears a slight crunch (crack), and the slender stem falls severed to the ground, totally harmless. The sun has become stronger and Jacinto, caressed by its rays, begins to feel calmer. As he works he has no visibility and cannot even, though he stands on tiptoe, see the ruined mill or the beehives or the reddish plowed earth; apart from the hedge, Jacinto can scarcely make out the stand of young trees behind the hut and, opposite it, the upper part of the oak grove and the top edge of the boulder (with its blackish-yellow caves and hollows) on the other side. His eagerness to rediscover the world imparts speed to his task, though from time to time he interrupts it to pile the cut branches at the base of the hedge. The work goes fast and, as his anxiety diminishes, he asks himself things like, for instance, how many days he can have been ill, and as just then he spots the treecreeper and sees it, teet-teet, slip into a crack in the shed, he concludes that the fever can't have lasted ten days, since the bird isn't carrying food in its beak and, consequently, can't have hatched its eggs. (This deduction of Jacinto's is arbitrary because he knows neither the day the eggs were laid nor the hatching period of treecreepers.) At intervals, Jacinto steps back a couple of meters to enjoy the effects of his pruning. He smiles. An empty space has been opened in the matted surface which shows that the gate is there, though imprisoned by stems and branches. However, Jacinto can reach it (the gate) by forcing himself sideways into the mass of foliage, and can even move it within the limited compass allowed to its hinges by the plant stumps.

When Jacinto has finished with the leafy parts (of the hedge) he starts on the tougher branches, and in this phase of the work it often happens that they resist the cutting pressure of the shears, and though Jacinto resorts to the help of his other hand, they refuse to fall. At such moments his (Jacinto's) dismay begins to return, as well as the sensation of anxiety in his diaphragm, and to still these feelings he (Jacinto) pretends not to notice, departs from his real objective and amuses himself by cutting the leafy parts around the edges, crick-crack, not essential for achieving his objective, pretending that he is doing something, although his (Jacinto's) head is buzzing with this idea: "You're really up a tree," which is strictly and rigorously true, but he (Jacinto) rejects it, moving his head from side to side as he often does when assailed by a sinful thought. And so he reaches an impasse in which he makes no more progress because all the branches between him and the gate do not yield to the repeated crunchings of the shears. He (Jacinto) summons up his courage and falls upon them violently, placing the blades in the grooves traced by his previous attempts and, after arduous efforts, which leave a painful imprint on his hands, manages to cut through two of them, which leads him to exclaim, "This is working." The knowledge that he still has in reserve instruments more expeditious than the shears instills a feeling of confidence in him, but he puts off using them (the instruments in reserve) so as not to destroy this comforting feeling, but finally, faced with the stubborn resistance of the five main branches and the stump (which has unexpectedly veered to the right and is blocking the gate), he lays the (now useless) shears on the ground, seizes the saw, sets it on the fork of one of the branches and moves it this way, scritch, that way, scratch, this way, scritch, that way, scratch, this way, scritch, that way, scratch, and, when he stops, he observes that the teeth (of the saw) are not penetrating the wood, that they have scarcely made a mark on the outer skin of the branch. He (Jacinto) then changes branches and concentrates his effort on a lower branch which allows him to put the whole weight of his body on it and thus to increase its (the saw's) power of penetration. It (the saw) has never been used before and traces of solid grease—the better to preserve it—can still be seen on both sides of the shiny white blade, but despite its good quality and Jacinto's doughty attack, scritch-scratch, scritch-scratch, the branch, perhaps because it is too soft and very rich in sap, rejects the saw, is so resistant that its teeth barely pierce the surface of the outer skin. Jacinto keeps trying a couple of times, and at last, convinced that it is useless, gets the idea of fastening the saw to the sole of his shoe, for in his zeal to try to excuse his impotence, he concludes that he hasn't enough muscle in his arms, for an expert calligrapher needs sensitivity in his hands but not strength and, also, the scratching of pen on paper, scree-scree, even if it is a continuous exercise (for days, and hours, and weeks, and even years), isn't exactly the sort of gymnastics to develop the biceps (Jeez, look what a bump Susanita just raised!). So he grabs a piece of cord and ties the saw edgewise to the sole of his shoe, but scarcely has he set its teeth on the forked branch and pressed down, than the saw blade ceases to be vertical and falls over, splat, against the sole of his shoe, and he (Jacinto) straightens it violently, awkwardly, and presses down once more, but it falls over again, splat, and on the third try the cord breaks and although Jacinto shrinks from bad language, he exclaims mechanically, beside himself, "Mother-fucker," he exclaims, though he knows perfectly well that saws are not fruit of the womb nor, consequently, children of mothers, but he says to it, "Mother-fucker," and although this relieves him for a moment, he soon feels guilty about it.

In view of his failure, Jacinto grabs the saw and returns to the charge, scritch-scratch, accumulating all his energies in his hands (though these energies become weaker and weaker), but the branch has too much sap in it and the saw barely frays the fibers at the fork in the branch. Beginning with this new attempt, Jacinto becomes quite desperate, turns his back on systematic efforts, climbs into the open space between the branches and begins to kick furiously, stamp-stamp, at the lowest branch until it bends, breaks, pop, but its outer skin is terribly tough and he has to swing on it (the branch) more than fifty times to break it off. Immediately, convinced of the efficacy of brute force, he tries to do the same with another large branch, but this one is so long that when he tries to twist it to loosen the outer skin, the end of it bumps into the branches above and the branches below and, to avoid this, he cuts it (the branch he is trying to break off) with the shears, crick-crack, but there still isn't room to move it, it's impossible to swing it, and he has to use the saw, scritch-scratch, to cut it. Jacinto swears, pants, but he is not intimidated. He is trying to open a clear path to the gate before he goes to bed, but whether the sun is moving too fast or he (Jacinto) too slowly, the fact is that by the time the enormous red disk is low over the hills, Jacinto has not yet succeeded in severing the third of the five branches that are in his way and, convinced of the need to do so, he twists it furiously, makes it swing from one side to the other, pulls on it, attacks it with the shears, dents it with the saw, clenches his teeth, utters short prayers, repeats in an access of fury, in a perfectly audible voice. "Motherfuckers all of you" (the branches), and when, after an hour of arduous efforts, he succeeds in tearing it off, he

112

examines the shredded stump and talks to it (the stump) as if it were a person: "Wow, how you hang on, you poor things!" he says, and finally he tosses the branch onto the refuse pile, straightens up little by little to alleviate the pain of his stiff back muscles, and immediately goes to work again.

At the instant the sun disappears behind the mountain a startling phenomenon occurs: the petals of the yellow flowers fold up as if protecting the stamens and, simultaneously, they begin to exhale a sweetish, concentrated, dizzying odor, mingling whiffs that resemble the smell of honeysuckle and roses, but stronger, so much so that they drown out the odors of thyme and lavender which prevail in the ravine. From the uplands descends the mournful twilight cry of the curlews, coo-ree, coo-ree, and in the thick leafage of the hedge the finches, the blackbirds, the grosbeaks, the wrens, the sparrows, the nightingales flit and sing, trui-chwick-tit-tit-orr-sib-sab, in a deafening cacophony. Jacinto feels suffocated by the intensity of the odor, the birds' clamor excites him and, having proved the uselessness of the pruning shears and the saw, and also having observed the progress of the night, he takes the axe and, beside himself, begins to hack away at the branch, whack-whack, but the branch seems to be made of rubber and rejects the blade as if it were a ball, and not even the slightest scratch appears on its surface, and Jacinto, maddened, begins to flail away at the hedge without trying to find a vulnerable place, right and left, without looking at what he is doing, hurting his hands and forearms, but ninety percent of the blows miss their mark and fall uselessly into the foliage

113

with a soft, bland impact, plaff, which contrasts with the sharp sound, tack, made by the blade every time it connects with the wood. Jacinto, possessed by a somber fury, does not stop to test the progress of his work. Overhead, the dazzling brilliance of the star Arcturus appears, and the birds fall silent and, in contrast, the bats begin to flit in bold swoops around Jacinto who, exhausted, stops, pants, haaa, haaa, grabs the branch, tries to twist it, and the branch bends elastically over the deepest gash but does not come loose, there even comes a moment when Jacinto, calling upon his last stores of energy, manages to touch the upper end of the branch to the fork where it begins, but in view of the fact that this is useless he (Jacinto) lets go of it, so awkwardly that the branch, as it swings back to its original position, strikes him violently on the chin and Jacinto staggers, is about to fall, and, still squatting, covers his eyes with his hands and begins to cry bitterly as he murmurs, "I'm shut in; this is an unbreakable blockade!"

"Blockade," he (Jacinto) said, and placed the two red pieces on the safety space, one beside the other, taking care to line them up evenly, while Doña Palmira clapped, clap-clap-clap, and said, "Now you're all going to see what kind of a player I am," and Doña Presenta, after examining the position of the four blue pieces, announced, "It's not fair, Jacinto, nobody can get the idea out of my head that you have something against me," and Señorita Josefita smiled, and when she smiled the crow's feet at the corners of her eyes got deeper, but this did not make Jacinto think that she (Señorita Josefita) was

114

old but that her skin was as fine and delicate as cigarette paper.

Doña Palmira, Doña Presenta, Señorita Josefita, and Jacinto were ensconced under the red-fringed lampshade, pulled so low that the lighted circle was concentrated on the multicolored parcheesi board, leaving the backs of the chairs, the sideboard, and the glass-fronted china cupboard in peaceful shadow. After two years of strict mourning, it was the first time that Señorita Josefita was playing with the yellow pieces, for, according to Doña Presenta, yellow was half-mourning, and Señorita Josefita said, "You'll see, I'm going to be terrible," and Doña Palmira agreed, "Señorita Josefita, anyone can see that yellow's not your color." Despite this, Señorita Josefita kept advancing with her leading piece and getting closer and closer to Doña Presenta's blue chip, immobilized by Jacinto's red blockade and, when she had nearly caught up with it, Doña Presenta grabbed Jacinto's forearm convulsively and said, "For the love of God, Jacinto, open up! open up! can't you see that they're already there?" but Jacinto was watching Señorita Josefita out of the corner of his eye and was moved by her skinny, defenseless forty-year-old body, her scarcely audible falsetto voice, her reddish eyelids that produced the impression that she had spent a lifetime crying, and "Five," said Jacinto, and "Come on, I've got all my pieces out," and he persistently rubbed one hand over the other and Doña Presenta closed her eyes, squeezing her eyelids together hard, and said, "These blockades really upset me, Jacinto, believe me," and Señorita Josefita shook the dice cup, yellow, porr-porr-porr, with her bony little hand, while Doña Presenta, hunched over the playing board, tried to ward off the danger, "Two, two, two!" she kept saying, and the yellow die showed a two and Doña Presenta clapped, clap-clap-clap, and "There's nothing like having confidence," she said, but Señorita Josefita warned her, "Don't count your chickens, Doña Presenta," and Doña Presenta turned to Jacinto, clutched his forearm, rolled up her eyes, and implored him, as if she really felt pursued by flesh-and-blood creatures, "Open up, Jacinto, I beg you in the name of the Most Holy Virgin!" but you would have thought Jacinto was made of ice, he lifted the dice cup and tipped it, thunk, "Three," he said, and moved up the piece that he had just taken out of the entrance space, and meanwhile Doña Presenta scolded him, "Well, I see that you don't ever mean to take that disgusting wall away from there," an obsession, until Doña Palmira got annoyed and said, "Either you shut up or we'll stop playing, Presenta; a game's only a game, anyone knows that," and at that instant Señorita Josefita rolled her die noisily, trinnnn, on the glass table top and exclaimed triumphantly, "One!" and, triumphantly, moved Doña Presenta's blue piece back to its corner and Doña Presenta said to Jacinto under her breath, "This was what I was afraid of; you're so stubborn that I knew it had to turn out badly," and eager to retaliate, Doña Presenta took off with her second piece, her eyes shining with anxiety, after Señorita Josefita's yellow one which had just captured hers and said, "Now you're going to pay me back everything at once, Josefita," but, right afterwards, Jacinto got a four and opened the blockade and immediately tried to justify himself with Doña Presenta, "If I move the other one, Doña Palmira's going to capture my piece," he said with a rabbity snicker, but Doña Presenta climbed up on her high horse and, "If we're going to start playing favorites it's no use," she said disenchantedly, "just look, opening the blockade now, and what I say is, if we're playing partners you ought to say so from the start," and she went on and on, and Señorita Josefita, all red with embarrassment, listened expressionlessly to the verbal battle, her eyes downcast, humiliated by the light from the red-fringed lamp, her skinny little hands resting on her lap, and just as Doña Palmira interrupted in her most thunderous voice, "For heaven's sake, Presenta, a game's a game!" and then, softening her voice, "It's your turn, Señorita Josefita," as soon as she said that, Señorita Josefita took the yellow cup, shook it, porr-porr-porr, turned it over, thunk, and made the die roll out on the glass table top, trinnnn, happy to be able to distract attention to the hopping die, and "Six!" said all four at once, and Doña Presenta, disappointed, "Go on, you'll never make it," and Señorita Josefita tipped the dice cup again, thunk, and another six came out, and "Six!" said all four of them at once, and Doña Presenta's expression of disappointment changed to a hopeful scowl and Señorita Josefita, as she shook the yellow dice cup, porr-porr-porr, for the third consecutive time, said, "It'll be bad luck too," and the four pairs of eyes followed the bouncing die and when it stopped Doña Presenta, on her feet, thundered out, "Six and things! God's trap always sings!" *but you know it's not like that, Jacinto, I'll* say, you know it, my boy, sometimes it sings and other times it doesn't, because if that weren't so, then all that stuff about ordeals and judgments of God would be fair, and they aren't, what the heck, the trap sings if it wants to, Jacinto, you know it all too well, the trap is just like a canary in a cage, it sings or it doesn't sing, the human condition is something else, Jacinto, that's a horse of a different color, I'll say, there's really no cure for that, what you win in life is won at the expense of someone else, for sure, that's what I say Jacinto, what the dickens could I do to make Doña Presenta and Señorita Josefita, both of them, go home happy after playing parcheesi? Nothing, Jacinto, don't bother your head about it, stop thinking ("Once more, once more!" yelled his office-mates) about it, you do somebody a favor and you make somebody else mad at you, life's like that, there's no doubt ("Once more, once more!") about it, if you intercede for ge-naromartín you're harming Darío Esteban, and if you don't do it, you're benefiting Darío Esteban and harming genaromar-tín, but you did intercede, I know that, I'll say I do, what're you going to tell me, and all for what? Let's be honest, Jacinto, because it seemed fair and reasonable to you, but look, you try that tack, my boy, and ask: what is fair? what is reasonable? come on, only out of curiosity, ask, Jacinto, a survey or whatever it's called, do it just for the pleasure of seeing if two people agree, only two, because I can tell you right now that they won't, because what's fair and reasonable has to be adjusted to what's mine, and if it doesn't adjust to what's mine, then it's neither fair nor reasonable, all that's like history and like words, Jacinto, each man controls his history and his words, and, because they're his, he can play fancy tricks with them if he wants to, to adjust them to

118

whatever he wants, Jacinto, you can be sure of that, because do you know what's the matter with history? well, there's only one thing the matter, that it's written by people who're alive, Jacinto, that's right, history ought to be written by dead people, but there's a difficulty about that, Jacinto, you know? because their hands are so cold they can't even grab the penholder, they don't know how, but that's what I say, Jacinto, why don't we teach them to write? We'd be doing a good work, I assure you, of course I know it'd be a nuisance at the beginning, we'd have to lead them by the hand and all that, the way they do with people who're dying and want to take their money out of the bank, I understand, a nuisance, but with a little patience maybe we'd get somewhere, why not? and after all, we wouldn't lose anything by trying, you can see that, because if not, the living come and tell you "All us men are equal; Christ said so," that's what they say, but that doesn't prevent some men from throwing other men to wild beasts, or into dungeons, or the gas ovens, and besides, and this is the funny part, they'll prove to you that that's the fair and reasonable thing to do, Jacinto, and maybe it is, it's anybody's guess, or maybe it's that men aren't equal, how do I know! or that we have two faces, or three, or four, a summer one and a winter one, how about it, now you take Don Abdón's speeches, applause, bravos, just fine, all congratulations, and then Amando García behind his back, Horny Otis this and Old Palindrome that, so where does that leave us? It's just like the part about the swimming pool and the bass drum, Jacinto, here between us, speaking perfectly frankly, do you think Don Abdón knows how to swim? Try to understand me, and don't go looking for trouble, Jacinto, I'm not trying to hint that Don Abdón isn't worthy of our

119

esteem, because Don Abdón is the most motherly father of all fathers, that goes without saying, and his relieving you of responsibilities is something money can't buy, I'll say, just try and buy it, Jacinto, but setting that aside, speaking perfectly frankly, he doesn't know how to swim, and as for the bass drum, Jacinto, not a bit of it, why deceive ourselves, and even supposing, and that's quite a suppose, that he did know how, Jacinto, even accepting the fact that he was a virtuoso, and that's quite an acceptance, do you think that a bass drum all by itself can produce music? Tell me the truth, Jacinto, honestly, can a bass drum produce music? Then why so much applause and so much fuss, Jacinto, would you like to explain that to me? And if people have two faces, or three, or four, which one is the good face? The summer one or the winter one? What a mess, Jacinto, and the fact is you have to get wise, men aren't equal, not even at a distance, and you'll say "They're not Christians," but they'll start bragging right away: "I'm a Christian by the grace of God," and the guy who says it lolls back on the seat of the rickshaw, yells, "Giddap!" and gives him a crack with the whip to get him going, and his equal, the man who's pulling the rickshaw, shuts his trap and off he goes and you think, "Tomorrow they'll change places; the one who's pulling will loll back and the one who's lolling back today will pull," but tomorrow is today by now and the one who's lolling back is the same one as yesterday, Jacinto, and he yells "Giddap!" again at the other one, and gives him a crack with the whip to get him going, and though they're equal they never change with each other, Jacinto, that's the joke, because to the one on the seat who tells you "I'm a Christian by the grace of God," it seems fair and reasonable that his equal should pull the rick-

*shaw while he lolls in the back, and as for the one who's
pulling, who knows, Jacinto, maybe he thinks something different but hasn't a voice, or if he has one his words are poor,
they're valueless, or maybe they're rich but, in this case,
they don't mean, you can be sure of that, the same as the
words of the guy who's lolling on the seat, and, therefore,
the one who's lolling doesn't understand him, can't understand him, and besides he has the whip, that's the serious
part, and, consequently, it's no use for the other one to talk,
and, therefore, it's better to shut up,* and he (Jacinto) makes
an effort, changes position and says nothing, though the
palms of his hands are burning, blisters have come out
on them, rings of raw flesh have appeared and he (Jacinto) carefully loosens the little circles of hardened skin
and, carefully, puts the tip of his tongue under them and
licks the sore places again and again. He (Jacinto) also
notices a painful sensation of tiredness halfway down his
thigh; and, above his buttocks, where he has been told
his kidneys are, it feels as if the axe blows had been delivered on him, down there, instead of his (Jacinto's)
having delivered them on the hedge and it feels as if he
had a deep gash on each side, like those trees that the
woodcutters leave hanging by a thread so that the lum-
bering team can pull them down, tying them with a rope,
one by one, next day (division of labor). The fact is that
Jacinto is wide awake, his eyes like saucers, the portable
lamp on the night table, and his thoughts skip capri-
ciously from pain to pain: hands, thighs, kidneys, biceps
(Jeez, look what a bump Susanita just raised!), kidneys,
and, at each thought, he changes position, but if he lies
face down his kidneys feel better but the pain in his

thighs and palms gets worse, and if he lies face up, the prickling of his blistered hands and the pain in his thighs is less but the pain in his kidneys gets worse, and if he lies on his right side, the pain in his left kidney and his left biceps and the thigh on the same side and even, with a little luck, the pain of his sore hands all get better, but on the other hand the pains in the right kidney, the right biceps, and the right thigh all come back, but if he lies on his left side, the pains in his right thigh, kidney, and biceps get less but the discomfort of his left thigh, kidney, and biceps gets proportionately worse. And every time he moves, Jacinto accompanies himself with an "ouuuch" in a more or less complaining and prolonged tone according to the time it takes him to change position, but, after the automatic, purely routine "ouuuch," he thinks that, no matter how he shuffles them, of the eight pains he suffers from (two hands, two kidneys, two thighs, and two biceps) he can't eliminate more than five and the rest, the other three, will continue whether he likes it or not. And the more he moves, the more conscious he (Jacinto) is of his pains and tells himself, "You're out of sorts, Jacinto. Rather than pain, the trouble with you is you're out of sorts." And because he acts on impulse, he stretches out one arm, opens the drawer of the night table, takes a bottle out of it, unscrews the top with one hand, takes out a sugar-coated pink pill, replaces the top on it (the bottle), closes the drawer, places the pill on the back of his tongue (underneath the uvula), picks up the glass, takes a mouthful of water and swallows it (the pill), glug. Immediately he hears a noise on the roof, a long-drawn-out, rhythmic noise, tap-tap-

122

tap, as if fingers were tapping on the slate shingles. At first the tapping is separate, tap-tap, but it grows faster and faster and in a few seconds has become a persistent and undifferentiated noise, whoooooof, which comes not only from the roof but from the garden, the elm trees, the hedge, the ravine, and the uplands. "It's raining," says Jacinto, suddenly catching on and, for the moment, he does not know whether the fact that it is raining is good or bad, he is vaguely aware that the rain is a novelty and that that constant and exhilarating noise (Jacinto has already forgotten about the pill) has calmed him, is making his eyelids heavy and is leading him, inevitably, toward sleep.

When he awakes, he hears the blackbirds calling, tchink-tchink-tchink, or, when he hears the blackbirds calling, tchink-tchink-tchink, he (Jacinto) awakes and, by the light that filters through the slats of the blind, he (Jacinto) deduces that the sun has come up. He sticks one hand out of the covers and pulls on the cord (of the blind), ra-ta-bla, and when he does so, along with the light, the burning sensation in his right hand, the pain in his right biceps, the stabbing pains in his right and left kidneys, and the violent contractions in his thighs (right and left) also awake in him. However, he jumps out of bed, sticks his bare feet into his shoes, puts his bathrobe on, and steps outside, fastening his belt as he goes. A strong odor of damp earth envelops him and in the blue of the sky, above the soaring vultures, he sees the white clouds rushing by, the last remnants of the storm. When he lowers his eyes, he (Jacinto) forgets everything else and sees only the hedge, an exuberant hedge which is now higher than his (Jacinto's) head, and whose leaves show clean, shining edges, in contrast to the dusty yellow of the flowers. Jacinto's heart beats in his chest, tick-tack-tick, when he moves toward the open space he had made last night next to the gate, and it speeds up, to the point of actually hurting him, when he sees that the open space scarcely exists. The tall branches of the hedge drip, plip-plop, on the lower ones and in the shadow of the lower branches the undergrowth is starting: the incipient fans of ferns, the spirals of creepers, the prickliness of nettles . . . The ground underneath shows the swarming porosity of worms and slugs characteristic of age-old forests. On the branches of the hedge that have been attacked by the axe, a few haphazard roots spring up and wave about seeking something to cling to, while the intact stems give birth to stalk-like roots along with leafy new branches, which completely conceal the log gate. Jacinto is stunned. He observes in astonishment the rapid progress of the creeping branches supported by the runners, the extraordinary expansion of the leaf buds, the swelling of the bulbs ready to explode. He (Jacinto) whirls around and sees that, within his whole visual field, the height of the hedge is surprisingly uniform. He seems to be unworried but, suddenly, shouts: "It's an unbreakable blockade! I'm a prisoner!" he cries, and the ravine answers "ner" and Jacinto starts to run aimlessly, back and forth, all the way around the cabin, his blue eyes bulging, he jumps up and down, waves his arms, while he thinks, "Prisoner; I'm a prisoner!" and, when he stops at last, his head seems on fire, his features contract in spasmodic grimaces and, after a short hesitation, he goes to the back of the cabin and returns with the axe, the adze, and the hoe, spits on the palms of his hands that are all broken out with blisters, seizes the hoe and begins to hack wildly at the new growth which separates him from the gate. His (Jacinto's) blows are soft and useless, thwack, thwack, and do no more than scare off dozens of birds and knock the heads off a few flowers, and, when he notices this, Jacinto flings the hoe against the side of the cabin, plunk, makes amends for his angry movement with a short prayer, runs like an automaton to the back of the hut, clambers up on the shed for the motor, takes firm hold of the eaves, flexes his arms, supports himself on his belly, draws up one knee and then the other and crawls along the slate shingles, desperately clutching the overlaps so as not to fall off the steeply sloping roof. When he reaches the chimney he grabs it and stands up and looks all around, and when he again sees the brook, the oak grove, the ruins of the mill, the patches of grama grass among the beehives, the red plowed earth, his eyes fill with tears. The hedge that cuts him off from that world is now more than six meters thick, and from up above Jacinto can see that it has a turflike and invulnerable texture. In an abrupt impulse, motivated by the knowledge that for every minute he delays flight will be more difficult, Jacinto takes a running start off the roofline, bounces twice on the steep slope, and as he reaches the eaves, jumps as far as he can, leaps into thin air, tries to make a double scissors kick in the air as athletes are said to do in the broad jump, and falls, whomp! on the tangled hedge which, within a few seconds, swallows him like quicksand. Jacinto kicks and struggles in the thicket, without result, yells "Help me!" and the ravine mocks him, "me" and again he yells "Help me!" and the ravine answers "me" and Jacinto keeps on making swimming motions with his arms, trying to disentangle himself from the shoots and branches that are holding him down, which keep him from moving his legs or wind themselves tightly around his chest and stomach and make breathing difficult. Jacinto is lying on his back, he feels himself held by the waist and thinks of a mosquito caught in a spiderweb, but, little by little, kicking furiously, he succeeds in recovering a vertical position, gets a foothold in the sturdy bend of a branch, pushes his body upward and, at last, his head emerges from the foliage and as he looks around he becomes demoralized, for, despite his titanic efforts, he has barely managed to get through a meter and a half of hedge and his situation, even if he wants to return to the cabin, is seriously endangered. He (Jacinto) tries to fight clear of the upper branches by making swimming motions, but the growth clings so tightly that he has the impression of being nailed down. Then, in the grip of a nervous crisis, he sets his entire body in motion, supports himself on his feet, hands, elbows, bottom, and knees to free himself from the clinging foliage, but the hedge holds him back with its thousand tentacles, holds him firmly, and he (Jacinto) screams and cries and if, at times, he is slow to move one of his limbs (an arm, for instance), for a few seconds the sharp little claws on the stems, avid to find something to attach to, twist around it, curl around it, dig their tiny stingers into the fabric of his bathrobe and begin to climb up it

126

as if they wanted to devour it, and, in those cases, Jacinto pulls them off with obvious repugnance, with flinching fingers as if he were pulling off poisonous snakes, and he yells and the echo yells too, and again he has the sensation of being a mosquito trapped in a spiderweb and notices the shivers running up and down his spinal column, convinced of the hedge's man-eating propensities. However, his efforts correspond to no plan, they are awkward and nervous, he kicks and moves his arms (Now in the deep end, Don Abdón!) without any method at all, desperately, and his very tension makes him unable to do anything and wears him out and there are moments when, conscious of his impotence, he is tempted to give up the fight and let himself die there. At these times he does not move, gasping painfully, haaa-haaa, but the sticky touch of a stamen or leaf on his neck or cheek is enough to make Jacinto straighten up again, to rebel, and then he bubbles with increasing energy and hostility, breaks off stems with kicks, rides on the hedge's surface for a few centimeters (almost endangering his masculinity), tears away the stems that are hindering the movement of his knees, slaps the nearest flowers whose petals and corollas are spread all over the solid surface of the hedge and his (Jacinto's) lips, usually virginally pure, mingle prayers for help with a few obscenities that rise involuntarily to his lips.

Sometimes Jacinto loses his footing, the bend or fork of the hedge fails him and he is again submerged in that vegetable sea and observes that he is asphyxiating and moves his arms and groans until he comes to the surface again and then he sighs deeply, but as night falls, and the yellow petals close over the stamens and the enervating odor of the flowers begins to spread, Jacinto thinks that the end has come, but he tries not to give in, he rejects the intoxicating perfume and yells "Damn you!" with all his heart and soul and, with his yell, discovers that his own voice encourages him and repeats "Damn you!" and the ravine answers "ooo!" and then he yells "Open up!" and the ravine replies "up!" and then he yells "I didn't want to ask anything!" and the ravine answers "ing!" and then he yells "I didn't mean anything bad by it!" and the ravine answers "it!" and then he (Jacinto) yells "I swear to God!" and the ravine answers "od!" And as he yells, Jacinto pedals away on the bends and stems, makes his fingers bleed, scratches his thighs, takes the skin off his elbows and forearms, hurts his testicles, and a white, expressionless moon observes him mockingly from the head of the valley, but he (Jacinto) doesn't give up, he contorts his body and every time his feet connect with a solid point of support, he pushes forward with all his strength, taking no notice of the scratches on his chest and belly, and during one of these efforts the hedge's resistance unexpectedly gives way and Jacinto falls violently, flat on his face, onto the paving stones, laughing and crying, barefoot, his bathrobe and pajamas ripped to pieces, his body bleeding, but he laughs and laughs, louder and louder, without the strength to get up; he stares at the moon and its quiet and self-satisfied fullness reminds him of Darío Esteban's quiet and self-satisfied face and, lying on the paving just as he is, he cups his hands to his mouth and screams desperately, "Darío Esteban, open the door!" and instantaneously the ravine answers "oor!" and Jacinto shouts, "I can't stand it any more!" and the ravine answers "ore!" and, suddenly, Jacinto gets to his knees, groans, opens his mouth and begins to laugh under his breath, dementedly, in bursts, drooling, rubs one hand against the other without noticing the stinging of the cuts and blisters, trembles, stands up and says ever so quietly, "A poem! Jacinto, you've made a poem!" he says with infinite pleasure and laughs again deep in his throat, as if he were gargling, "A poem," he repeats, "Darío Esteban, open the door, I can't stand it any more," he murmurs as he walks, staggering like a drunkard, into the cabin and lights the kerosene lamp and he (Jacinto) collapses into a chair and bursts out sobbing bitterly, and in the short pauses between his sobs, repeats, "A poem, now I know how to make poems," and he dries his tears with the backs of his hands and, as he raises his eyes, is astonished at the neatness and silence that prevail in the cabin and the antelope, from the chimney piece, stares at him with its impassive glass eyes and Jacinto stares back at it, and tells it, "Now I know how to make poems," and bursts out into bubbling laughter.

His muzzle was stubby and black and comma at the end of it comma the clearly defined holes comma like musical notes comma and the look in his hazel eyes watchful and alert as if he were still alive period The short stiff hair on the head became thicker at the ears comma where the graceful curve of the neck began comma brutally slashed by the knife blade at the point where the brown blot on the thorax began spreading over the back to the hindquarters period The ceiling of the room was high and the walls white and bare with large Gothic windows comma with no inside shutters or curtains comma open to the darkness of the night and over the long white marble table floated five globes of light comma whose studied arrangement eliminated all shadows period There was a strong smell of carbolic acid and after the dry and deliberate noise of footsteps along the long bare corridor click-click-click comma the silence of the room became especially thick period The head was resting on the clean cut made by the knife and a thin trickle of almost black clotted blood was spreading along the marble end of paragraph

The woman comma motionless and silent up to that point comma put her handkerchief to her eyes comma then to her mouth and cried half-smothering the cry with her handkerchief Genaro, Genaro my darling! and the older doctor took her delicately by one arm and told her pull yourself together; we must be strong comma and immediately comma turned his head toward the younger doctor comma sheathed like him in a white lab coat comma and added in a whisper accompanied by an admiring gesture comma a beautiful pointer, isn't it?

Jacinto stops staring at the antelope's nasal orifices, stands up, goes into the kitchen and as he beats the eggs to make himself an omelet, it occurs to him that speech, with all its imperfections, can still be redeemed, that the urgent task is to find virgin words that suggest the same ideas in everyone's brain, but, all of a sudden, his thoughts take another turn, he stops beating the eggs, sets the bowl with the eggs in it on the stove and says to himself, "I'm boxed in; I can't waste any time." Si-

multaneously he observes that he is barefoot, his clothing is in rags, and his body covered with bruises. He
steps under the shower and cries aaaah! unable to stand
the stinging pain in silence, then he daubs himself with
Mercurochrome and dresses hastily and goes out into the
night, in his hand the kerosene lamp whose white flame
is immediately surrounded by moths and mosquitoes. He
(Jacinto) tries to breathe deeply of the cold night air and
exhale it in intermittent puffs, pssst-pssst, attempting to
moderate the beating of his heart which is bumping
frantically against his chest. He repeats the exercise four
or five times and, following that, leaves the lamp on the
ground and measures the distance between the two strips
of hedge: four long steps. However, the open space between the hedge and the cabin is less than a meter. "I
can't go to sleep without settling this," he tells himself.
He feels intuitively that to go to sleep under these circumstances can mean death and, on the other hand, activity will relieve the tension he feels. He (Jacinto) then
enters a phase of delirious agitation, under pressure his
brain brings forth conflicting ideas, he (Jacinto) bustles
to and fro, interrupts actions already begun, begins others, until at last he seems to make up his mind, enters
the cabin, goes down to the cellar and returns with a
large can of gasoline and two bottles of alcohol. He sets
everything down on the stones, near the door, and goes
out behind the hut to the toolshed. There the perfume of
the flowers is so honey-sweet and disturbing that Jacinto
is intimidated, and he hastens to return to the front sector and, with the rake, heaps the hedge cuttings beside
the gate, sprinkles the cut branches with gasoline and

131

alcohol, sets fire to them and steps back. The instant glare dazzles him and calms his nerves, gives him back confidence in his own efforts. The flames spiral upward, crackling, crip-crip, popping, pttt-pttt, until they are twice as high as the hedge, so voraciously that the stars in the sky are blotted out and Jacinto smiles faintly, fascinated by the spectacle. "It'll never stand up to this," he thinks, but his hopes vanish within a few minutes, for, far from growing as he had expected, the fire begins to languish, the flames fall back on themselves (as if they had been fed artificially) and slowly fade away, are extinguished, and nothing is left in their place but a dying bed of ashes. Jacinto goes closer and the smoke makes him cough. He looks around. Really, the hedge hardly shows the effects of the flames. Over a broad area the leaves are blackened and some of the branches (the most superficial ones) are scorched (so that they yield easily to pressure) but the main stems and deepest branches are still intact. "It's too damp," he (Jacinto) tells himself, and his heart starts its agitated beating again. But he is in a state of feverish excitement, his failures are a source of new initiatives and his (Jacinto's) aggressive ideas join together in increasingly strong links. While the ashes are still alive, Jacinto returns to the cellar and brings up, one by one, three bottles of gas which he places inside the hedge, making a hollow with the axe and pruning shears. Then he lays a cord soaked in gasoline one of whose ends he places in the spout of the gas bottle, which he has left open, sprinkles everything (gas bottles and hedge) with the gasoline and alcohol still left in their respective containers, lights the fuse and runs (lamp in hand) behind the cabin. Once there, he crouches between the house and the well, face down, literally stuck to the ground, his clutching hands protecting the back of his neck, his mouth open, his whole body tense . . . The explosion is so violent, boooooom! that he hears the kitchen window opening over his head (in a second, more muffled explosion, boooof, as if it had been unsuccessful) and shards and powdered glass rain down on his body, tinkle-tinkle-tinkle. His next impulse is to stand up, but he (Jacinto) hesitates, he (Jacinto) is assailed by the suspicion that the explosion of the gas bottles has not been simultaneous and so he stays quiet, without changing his position, waiting. But as the minutes go by Jacinto begins to feel more confident, first, he takes his hands away from his neck, closes his mouth, stretches his arms and legs, puts his head on one side, kneels, listens carefully (nothing can be heard), gets up, goes to the corner of the cabin and looks out furtively from among the branches as children do when they play cops and robbers. By the light of the flaming liquid, which is at its last gasp, he (Jacinto) observes that the gas bottles have disappeared but the hedge is still there, unchangeable, and, on the other hand, there are pieces of glass, chips of slate, and a twisted drainpipe scattered on the ground. As he moves toward the fire he sees the broken windows, opened wide by the explosion, and in the corner of the hut nearest the gate, the log siding has been torn off and the roof slates have fallen to the ground in pieces. But the hedge is untouched, solid and mute, offensive in its passivity, and Jacinto, after mentally cataloguing the destruction caused by the explosion, begins to measure the number of paces between the lateral strips of hedge and, either because his paces are now longer or because the hedge's progress has speeded up, no matter how many times he tries it he can't make it more than three and a half.

He (Jacinto) goes into the house feeling disconcerted, and the disorder there overwhelms him. He picks up the broom and sweeps conscientiously. When he has finished he closes the glassless windows, lets down the blinds, leaves the inside shutters ajar, sprawls in an armchair, uncorks a bottle and drinks in one interminable swallow. He doesn't really know what he is drinking, nor does he care, but the liquid produces a warm optimism in his belly, so welcome that it causes him to repeat the action until his optimism turns into euphoria and his euphoria into drowsiness. In the silence he hears the broken cry, goo-ek, of the nightjar on the road and the owl's short moan, kiu, in the top of the elm tree. Before he closes his eyes, Jacinto looks again at the antelope's head, its shiny glass eyes, and bursts out laughing.

"The Company is not trying to make things difficult for you and your children and is willing to consider that your husband died in line of duty. This is far from being true, dear lady, and you are not unaware of it, but I repeat that the company does not wish to make things difficult for you and is willing to consider a new view of the problem in exchange for your foregoing, dear lady, a religious burial for your husband and thus avoiding a conflict of jurisdictions. After all, dear lady, the earth is the same everywhere and unfortunately your husband can no longer take offense over it."

The woman bit her handkerchief comma after repeatedly rubbing it over her eyes and said please understand me comma after letting him die like a dog I can't resign myself to putting him underground like a dog; he didn't deserve this comma she said comma and Darío Esteban comma when he heard her say this comma leaned forward comma placidly interlaced the fingers of both hands and sat forward on the edge of the chair colon

"Of course I realize what your feelings are, dear lady, and in a certain sense I share them, but I know that this is the time to let the head speak, not the heart. Your husband, in case you are unaware of it, was not on the payroll in recent months but was, as the saying goes, paid under the table. The position, within the sub-subaltern job scale, was created for him, you understand, we made it up out of whole cloth, we invented it so that you and your children would not be without resources. Hence, if he is not on the payroll, he hasn't received a net paycheck and if he hasn't received a net paycheck the credit union and the insurance don't cover him, and if the credit union and the insurance don't cover him because your husband is not entitled to coverage, the problem is a problem of charity and comes down to this: either you continue to exert pressure on the ecclesiastical hierarchy to give him a religious burial, something which is in any case problematical and in view of which the Company washes its hands of the matter, or you accept our conditions in advance, in which case the Company is willing to concede that your husband died in line of duty (and if the attack had been perpetrated inside the fence it would have been, you understand), and will indemnify you on the basis of your husband's paycheck prior to his demotion and will even look out for your children when they are older. So that you will understand me, what the Company is trying to avoid is an overlapping of areas of responsibility."

Jacinto looked at the woman out of the corner of his eye and in view of the fact that she did nothing but hiccup and sob and did not answer comma he said excuse me for interrupting, Darío Esteban. The head, will you give us that too? and Dario Esteban comma before he comma Jacinto comma had finished speaking comma put his right hand into the inside pocket of his coat and took out some papers colon

"Excuse me," he added. "These two certificates were sent yesterday from the Don Abdón Institute. Your husband, dear lady, did not suffer from hydrophobia. I congratulate you, it has all been a false alarm. He enjoyed good health and his aggression resulted from a complicated process of emotional resentment and environmental pressures which it is not appropriate to discuss at the moment. I mean that your husband's act of aggression will not have consequences. On the other hand, and in view of the circumstances, neither can any responsibility whatever be imputed to the farmer: he acted in legitimate defense of his person and of his family; that is the law. As for your husband's head, dear lady, you can do one of two things: go and pick it up at the Don Abdón Institute on presentation of this ticket, or authorize Doctor Mateu in writing to have it stuffed. We men are mysterious creatures and apparently the doctor has taken a fancy to it and is willing to pay you a considerable sum for it."

136

Darío Esteban paused and the woman became impatient period Twice Jacinto seemed to want to say something but thought better of it and both times he opened his mouth and closed it again without managing to say a word end of paragraph

"As I understand it," continued Darío Esteban, "the option leaves no room for doubt, dear lady. You have the opportunity to pick up a nice piece of cash on condition that you give up consecrated ground on the one hand and your husband's head on the other. Keep one thing in mind: your husband's head isn't going to do either you or your husband any good, and, on the other hand, I'm sure that the doctor will compensate you generously and, moreover, and this is important, he will give you permission as long as your sense of loss persists, he will give you permission to visit it in his office on Thursday and Sunday afternoons after office hours. It's your choice."

"No!" shouts Jacinto angrily.

He is on his feet, his hair in disorder, his facial muscles convulsed, his pupils staring, he takes the chair by the back, lifts it with incredible ease and smashes it furiously against the stones of the chimney piece, where the beautiful antelope's head is hanging, which falls broken to the floor, while one of its glassy syrupy eyes rolls and rolls until it is hidden under the lowest shelf of the bookcase. "Five!" screams Doña Presenta. "Five and things, God's trap always sings!" but he, Jacinto, does not sing, in particular if there is some girl nearby, but pretends to sing; that is, he shapes his lips like someone who is singing but does not emit a single sound, he simply limits himself to nodding his head yes, not only to denote agreement with the statements of Don Abdón, seated like a Buddha, his breasts jiggling, with their black nourishing nipples, framed by the Solomonic columns of the golden baldachin, but to relieve his Adam's apple of that unbearable feeling of tension and relieve the weight of his head on the first cervical vertebra, and so he (Jacinto) assents without speaking, mute, because the muffler seals his lips and keeps him from talking and Darío Esteban, in an impersonal voice, persuasive in tone, tells him, "I want you to keep two things in mind: first, Darío Esteban has never said to breathe for Don Abdón or not to breathe, that is the option, and second: you people are not adding dollars, or Swiss francs, or kilowatt-hours, or blacks, or young ladies in nightgowns (white slave trade) but ADDENDS. I think the matter's perfectly clear," but it isn't clear to Jacinto, rather it's quite the opposite, its consistency is so thick that if he moves his arms energetically, the air serves to hold him up and he rises off the ground and, once he is floating in the air, it becomes easier for him to rise higher and even glide, and then, when he sees the petty crowd down below, restless and routine-ridden as ants in an anthill, he says in a tone of great conviction, "Neithe rheto nor diale; eve attem at comprensa through the spowo is a uto." Darío Esteban, in the center of the anthill, shakes his fist at him (Jacinto) and roars like a madman, "Are you trying to insinuate, Jacinto San José, that Don Abdón is not the most motherly father of all fathers?" but the farmer doesn't open his mouth, nor does he answer him (Darío Esteban), nor does he curse him (Jacinto), but confines himself to aiming at him (Jacinto), to following his

138

movements through the sights of the shotgun, calculating the distance and speed *grosso modo* and, almost without transition, fires off both barrels, almost without transition, and so Jacinto plummets down, Doña Palmira, solicitous as always, holds his head maternally by the nape of his neck and tells him, breathing right into his face, "What kind of a nest have you fallen from, Master Jacinto?" but the boy in the shooting gallery, when he hears the detonations, yells, "Prize for the young lady!" and the crowd presses around them and Señorita Josefita hops like a baby sparrow on the tips of her toes and claps, clap-clap-clap, and when they show her the dissident's shattered eye in a glass of water, she forgets her good manners and squeals, "The toffee, Jacinto! I've won a box of toffee!" And a great Hercules of a man with a lunchbox in his hand murmurs, "Shee-it, that's some eye they gave him; there's one guy who won't see straight again." And the glances of the whole crowd skewer him (Jacinto) like pins and as more and more of them push in, they crush him against the counter and Jacinto, half asphyxiated, sees no other solution than to climb up on it (the counter) and leaps over the crowd from there and tries to open a path with kicks and elbowings, but the humerus bones, and the femurs and the collarbones and the kneecaps and the finger joints and the anklebones of the spectators dig into him all over, they hamper his movements, and as he (Jacinto) realizes that he is in bad trouble he yells "Help!" and the ravine answers "elp!" but the doctor soothes him: "We're doing everything humanly possible," he says, placing a tepid hand on his forehead, and adds, "I presume that I owe you an explanation but this test is indispensable for me, believe me. The patient, by instinct, barricades himself behind what he believes to be his personality, but this does not exist, it is a mere potentiality. The patient, however, does not admit this because he is a vain, stubborn, and impervious being. To make him relax and to obtain a spontaneous reaction from him, we must previously have emptied him, depersonalized him, you do understand me, don't you?" Jacinto stands up. "To hell with logic, doctor, if your question is meant to be logical," he says, but Darío Esteban, always equal to the occasion, cuts him short. "Why are you talking foolishness, Jacinto San José? Talk about the catenaccio defense; sincerely, do you believe that the catenaccio defense will eventually destroy soccer as a spectacle?" Jacinto flees; again he moves his arms vigorously to overcome the resistance of gravity and rises slowly over the flowerbeds and borders of the park until his head brushes against the lowest branches of the chestnut trees, but when he feels the sharp pain in his biceps and the subsequent cramps, he cannot avoid a fall and closes his eyes, but the little old ladies seize him in their trembling interlaced hands and run like mad, carrying him, among the shifting lights of the flares and torches, singing tunelessly,

"Make a chair, make a chair,
for the queen with golden hair.
Comb it down, comb it down,
see the lice run around,"

and people applaud and yell bravos and say, "Jeez, look what a bump Susanita just raised!" and suddenly they

140

(the black-clad hundred-year-old women) stop, squat, stand up, tighten their skinny arms, yell in unison, "Upsy-daisy!" and toss him (Jacinto) into the air and Jacinto sees the pond underneath him and tries as hard as he can to adopt an insouciant (lighthearted, at least) attitude as he falls, but he can't manage it and plummets unsuccessfully (a bellywhop) onto the surface of the water in a comic dive. And instead of the laughter he expected he hears the enthusiastic, comforting ovation, from the shores of the lake and, after they have finished applauding, people cry, "With-out-the-life-ring, with-out-the-life-ring!" but Don Abdón interrupts and cuts them short: "Talking about sports is even healthier than practicing them," he tells him and Jacinto nods yes, inhibited by his swollen breasts (which have coneshaped nourishing nipples) and when he (Don Abdón) adds, "You're timid, Jacinto San José, aren't you?" Jacinto (San José) recognizes that he is, assents once more and in this way helps the tension in his neck and the numbness in his first cervical vertebra owing to the dead weight of his head, which was there, standing (the head) motionless on the immaculate whiteness of the marble, under the five incandescent globes, the pupils as alert as if he were still alive, and the older doctor turns to the younger doctor, who is also sheathed in a white lab coat, and says to him in a discreet whisper, "A beautiful pointer, isn't it?" Jacinto again nods yes, wordlessly, and Don Abdón takes advantage of his acquiescence to tell him, "The hedge is the defense of the timid."

Jacinto makes himself humble. Jacinto is humble in addition to being honest (his honesty is beyond all doubt). He is perhaps, today, the only man in the world who has only one thing to say, "Let's understand each other," and, therefore, he (Jacinto) thinks that the Tower of Babel could be the answer because "Let's understand each other" is something that can be said even without being spoken aloud, by signs, and this is the reason why he founds his movement "Through Silence to Peace," but, when he does it (founds the movement), he finds that keeping silent is not the same as speaking without being understood, that it may seem the same but it isn't the same, for man is not a rational animal, or if he is ("Let's say we admit it," thinks Jacinto), the condition of a talking animal predominates over the quality of being a rational animal, that is, he (man) needs to say things even though he doesn't think them through, he (man) needs to let off steam, to pretend that he (man) is reasoning even though he may do so by starting from false premises, and the better he pretends (that he is reasoning) the more satisfied he (man) is with himself, even though it be at the expense of chopping his neighbor into pieces or slandering him or cheating him, for this is secondary, since the essential thing is to let off steam (charity properly understood begins at home), and this is why Jacinto is a pitiable exception, a man (among billions of men) with nothing to say (except, as has been said, "Let's understand each other"), and hence (because he has nothing to say) he says nothing and if his officemates in the Refectory talk about sports and passionately discuss among themselves whether or not the catenaccio defense has ruined soccer as a spectacle, he (Jacinto) keeps quiet and only if the disagreement becomes heated does he pretend to put his oar in so as not to be impolite to them (his officemates), so as not to show indifference to the concerns of others, but it's the same as when he pretends to sing (if he puts his oar in, that is) and he only says, and repeats to the point of exasperation, "Well I say that the catenaccio defense, well I say that the catenaccio defense, well I say that the catenaccio defense," to the point of exasperation, like an automaton, yes, at the top of his voice, feigning an enthusiasm that he is very far from feeling, but, as the noise is very great, no one hears him, the only thing that is obvious is his aggressiveness and Jacinto, again and again, tries to pretend that he is saying something, but actually he isn't saying anything (like all the rest of them) except, "Well I say that the catenaccio defense, well I say that the catenaccio defense, well I say that the catenaccio defense," so as not to seem silent or stupid, or be different from the others, or show that he doesn't know his officemates' language, but one morning when he (Jacinto) butted into a discussion in which half a dozen of his officemates were talking at once, well I say that the catenaccio defense, well I say that the catenaccio defense, well I say that the catenaccio defense, suddenly there was a silence and you couldn't hear anyone's voice but his, well, that morning Ginés Gil turned to him, put a hand on his shoulder and said, "What have you got to say about the catenaccio defense, Jacinto San José?" and Jacinto, not knowing what to say, felt the blood rush to his head, but by a vulgar association of ideas he remembered Amando García, remembered his opinion about the bolt of the toilet (gentlemen)—catenaccio equals bolt—and as Ginés Gil returned to the charge, "What have you got to say about the catenaccio defense, Jacinto San José," he, Jacinto, said in a strangled voice, "I think it's a petit-bourgeois practice," and it was as if he had lighted the fuse of a bomb, all six of them yelled out their arguments again at the tops of their voices and by their wildly waving arms and the repeated claps on the back that Ginés Gil administered to him, Jacinto guessed that he had said something useful without knowing what he was saying and amid the confusion of words and exclamations he half-heard Ginés Gil say, "That's right, a viciously conservative attitude," and he smiled, but since Ginés Gil kept on slapping him on the back as if encouraging him to support him, Jacinto spoke again to say, over the inextricable knot of his officemates' argument, "Well I say that the catenaccio defense, well I say that the catenaccio defense, well I say that the catenaccio defense," like a cracked record, and when the bell rang and all conversations broke off abruptly, Ginés Gil underscored his admiration by giving him a final slap on the back and saying, "That's it, you said it, Jacinto's right this time."

And when his (Jacinto's) idiosyncrasy was transferred to the sentimental area, it didn't do him any good either, for all the girls he has known (including Señorita Josefita with her silky skin and her crow's feet) seem to him (Jacinto) more at ease and intelligent than he, or, at least, the things they say or try to express seem witty and to the point and, if they don't say anything, they give him the (always favorable) sensation that they are thinking, that is, Jacinto inevitably gets the worst of things, for if the girls are talkative, he (Jacinto) keeps his

144

mouth shut for fear of competing with them in wittiness, aggressiveness, or intelligence, and if they say nothing he (Jacinto) speaks without using his brain (even though not very much, for he always speaks little), but everything he says is boring and trivial (just chatter pure and simple) and he thinks that she (the girl who isn't talking) is thinking that he (Jacinto), who is talking, is a perfect fool and if, on the other hand, the one who chatters is the girl (at top speed, of course) he (Jacinto) thinks that she (the girl) must think that he (Jacinto) has nothing to say because he's a born idiot. In short, that no matter how much he thinks about the question, he (Jacinto) can never come up with a satisfactory answer.

He (Jacinto) wakes up with a start, with a wry neck from his position in bed, and gets to his feet so quickly that he thinks he has been asleep that way (on his feet) and before he has time to figure this out he finds himself in the frost-wet outdoors just after daybreak, flanked by two walls of vegetation (more than two meters high), and his appearance on the scene is so rapid that the young rabbit surprised in the corner hardly has time to escape from the burrow it was trying to dig, and to dash headlong into the undergrowth. Despite the confusion in his brain caused by his headlong fall, this is a revelation for Jacinto. "Naturally," he (Jacinto) says. "It's as simple as Columbus's egg." (What the fuck, if old Gen hasn't eaten the country boy's things!) And so, the first stroke of the hoe, thunk, merely deepens the hole the rabbit has started to dig, and as he makes it (the stroke of the hoe), Jacinto thinks that with two or three hundred (maybe a thousand) strokes like that he can find his way to freedom. In view of this (adding up the possible number of efforts represents for Jacinto, who is used to making calculations, less effort than to make those efforts) Jacinto goes to work energetically, without thinking about his weakness, without noticing the creeping advance of the tendrils, solidly attached to the runners, ignoring the inclination of the two strips of hedge, mutually attracted to each other, which threaten to form a vegetal arch over his head. From time to time Jacinto spits on the palms of his hands, drops the hoe, seizes the shovel, and digs, from the trench he has made, more of the damp red crumbled earth, whose resistance to the steel blade becomes progressively less. "Half a meter square should be enough," thinks Jacinto, "though for the moment I ought to make it wider so I can move more freely." And he digs energetically and sweats and says to himself, "It's as simple as Columbus's egg," and, from time to time, he digs out the earth with the shovel and proudly surveys, passing the blue-veined back of his hand over his forehead, the heaps of reddish earth, growing higher and higher, which surround the hole on all four sides.

Suddenly he opens his eyes and sees the rectangle of sky, the whitish cirrus cloud cut off by the edge of the hole, a vulture gliding under it (under the cloud) and notices cold and wetness in his bottom and the handle of the shovel sticking into his lower back, hurting him; and he also sees the superposition of layers, of varying consistency and color, owing to the humidity and the quality of the earth and the odor of deep, just-turned earth reaches his nose, and he sees in the upper layers the little hanging roots of the thicket and the ends of the worms twisting and trying to hide, and the holes made by mole tunnels and the white stones encrusted between the layers. Jacinto sees and smells all these things, he is fully conscious of them, but he cannot coordinate the muscular movements necessary to stand up (which is what he wants to do) and he moves his elbows and legs but inevitably collides with the vertical walls of the hole and then, despite the fact that he sees the blue sky splendidly framed (like a picture) by the top layer, and the last fringes of the flying cloud, and the silent swoops of the vulture under them (under the fringes), despite all this, Jacinto thinks stupidly, "They've buried me alive." And he reacts violently to this conviction, stirs, manages to get on his knees inside the hole (the heaped-up earth still keeps him from seeing the cabin) and, with his elbows on the edge of the pit, he stands up and stays for several minutes in that position (standing with his elbows on the heaped-up earth), trying to reconstruct (without success) the immediate past, and at last, little by little, first raising one knee and then the other and crawling over the piles of dirt and gravel, centimeter by centimeter, he gets outside and breathes deeply and observes carefully the destruction caused by the explosion of the gas bottles (yesterday, day before yesterday, several weeks ago?) and as he reaches the cabin he grabs hold (as if they were stair steps) of the surviving logs and, although his arms tremble, he manages to pull himself upright and walks into the house dragging his feet, raises the blind and looks at himself in the mirror of the toilet (gentlemen) and as Jacinto mistily glimpses that waxen face, streaked with an unkempt yellow beard, his hair dirty and in disarray, his eyes staring above big purple bags, he tells himself, *Jacinto, just look at you, you poor guy, you look like a man who's been shipwrecked, my God, be careful now and don't lose your cool because if you lose your cool you're sunk and, after all, others are worse off than you are, Jacinto, for when all's said and done, plants are your friends, always, I certainly ought to know, to be besieged by plants is almost a good dream, I'll say, and if you start to think about it to die like this, hugged to death by flowers, is almost a poetic death, just imagine what it would be like to be hounded by minerals or hounded by animals, by men, for instance. Keep calm, Jacinto, what interest could I have in deceiving you, and in these circumstances, look, imagine that instead of a hedge it was two steel plates, what do you think of that? because after all, that's more or less what happens in a cruiser if an enemy torpedo comes along and boooom! sinks it, d'you realize that? And what happens then? Hold on a moment, Jacinto, I'm going to tell you about it, keep calm now, you'll see, there are a lot of people in the cruiser, some up above and some down below, some on deck, some in the turrets and the antiaircraft stations to port and starboard and in the machine-gun emplacements, and the bridge and the firing control positions, all right, those are up above, as I told you, but others are belowdecks, in the storerooms and the compartments, well and truly trapped by the watertight doors, closed under pressure, understand? like soda in a bottle, shut up tight as a drum, and they can't do anything unless their shipmates in the next compartment raise the door levers, but the shipmates in the next compartment won't raise the levers because, one or the other, they're dead or discipline keeps them from doing it,*

Jacinto, because discipline on a cruiser is very important, d'you realize that? I'll say, their only job is to control flooding, just think about that, and if they open the watertight doors the flooding will spread, so that if they can't open the watertight doors because discipline keeps them from doing it or they're dead, one or the other, and then the sailor in the compartment has to take what's coming and what's coming, Jacinto, is that the cruiser sinks, it inevitably goes down because the torpedo has made a direct hit, under the waterline, understand, and the cruiser starts to roll, first to one side, then to the other, and the sailors who were abovedecks when the order came for battle stations, either on deck or in the machine-gun emplacements, or in the firing control positions, as soon as they see that the cruiser is starting to roll, first to one side, then to the other, they take and jump into the water, see, what a mess, some in the lifeboats, others with life jackets on, fighting for all they're worth, and the one with no life jacket fights all the harder, they're stark naked, mother-naked, Jacinto, as the saying goes, but still struggling because what they have to do is swim as hard as they can (let's be honest, Jacinto, just between us, Don Abdón doesn't know how to swim), because if you don't swim as hard as you can, Jacinto, you run the risk of being pulled down by the whirlpool the cruiser makes when it sinks, see? of its sucking you in like a piece of fluff in the bathtub drain, and you go to the bottom like a stone . . . Keep calm, Jacinto, don't get impatient, your nerves are really on edge, the heck with you, nobody can hold you down, this happens with those who're abovedecks and some are saved and others drown, naturally, that goes without saying, see, but the others, those who are down there in the storerooms and com-

149

partments, they can't see the sky or the water, Jacinto, they see only the watertight doors and the portholes and the great strong rivets on the steel plates, get it? and then the only thing they can do is start listening, and, naturally, they listen as hard as they can and when they hear the guns firing, crump-crump-crump, and the explosion of the torpedo, boooom! and footsteps running overhead, thud-thud-thud, they think, "This is starting to look ugly." That's what they're thinking, for sure, Jacinto, it's anybody's guess though, maybe they think about their wives or about their children, good thoughts naturally, what did you imagine, but no matter what they think, as soon as the swaying begins and then the listing and then the lights go out (because everything has gradually stopped working, Jacinto, even though a few minutes ago the cruiser was a machine as accurate as a watch) and the ship goes down stern-first and the prow sticks up, think of that, and they roll over the floor and crash into the rail or the metal lockers or the bulkhead, it depends, Jacinto, then, as I'm telling you, they even stop listening, they just stay there huddled up, saying all the prayers they know, Oh Lord Jesus Christ, all the time the sinking lasts, which might be a long time or a short time, that's logical, depends on the depth, but I understand, Jacinto, just imagine that somewhere there are abysses of water six thousand meters deep, that's easy to say, six kilometers, Jacinto, that's really something, but because the ship sinks slowly you might spend ten minutes swaying there, hands clasped together and praying like mad, waiting, but really you're not waiting for anything, Jacinto, just waiting for the ship to settle on the bottom and after a bump it lies there quietly among the rocks and the algae and the coral. And once this happens the sailor goes and stands up and though he doesn't see a thing, he touches himself, pinches himself and knows that he's alive, though there's a silence like the tomb all around him, maybe with six kilometers of salt water over his head, maybe, but he knows he's alive and kicking (though he figures it's not for long), d'you get the picture? but he still has plenty of oxygen because the compartment is big and he can breathe and think (the bad part isn't the fly, Jacinto, but thinking about the fly) and even light a match and pull himself together. And, just imagine, by the light of the match the poor sailor sees the objects that up to a few minutes ago were the underpinnings of his daily life, of the routine he used to curse, that's something else again, Jacinto, that is, he sees the bench and the table where he put his tray down and ate scarcely an hour ago, and now they're fastened to the ceiling by two bars, and he sees the hooks where he fastened the ropes of his hammock to sleep till his replacement on watch woke him up and he also sees the warm corner under the pale light bulb in its wire cage where he used to sit (on the linoleum floor) every afternoon to read a Western, that is, so you'll get the picture, Jacinto, he sees everything intact (the torpedo opened the hole in the prow) and though everything's the same, everything's different, get it? and, for a moment, the sailor loses control of himself, Jacinto, which is the least he can lose under the circumstances, and he yells and howls and tears his hair and throws himself against the ship's side (made of steel plates ever so carefully riveted together in the shipyard) and bangs on it (the ship's side) with his clenched fists and, in view of its imperturbable resistance, the sailor does all his business, Jacinto, I mean, he shits and he pisses, until the pain (in his fists) brings him

151

back to reality, understand? and at that point the sailor takes
and says to himself, "Patience, Dick, others are worse off,"
d'you get the reference? for if a man can't find some consolation he's not really trying, Jacinto, my boy, and that's a
big fat truth, because the sailor, then, starts thinking about
the innocent people condemned to the gas chambers, are you
beginning to get the point? "To the showers, to the showers," they say and the jailers line everybody up and read the
list because everybody wants to take a shower and the
hundred who've been chosen yell "To the showers, to the
showers," and run toward the barracks, jostling one another,
because they can't wait to get their dirt-smeared and flea-
ridden bodies under the water and as soon as they get there
they turn the handles and stand mother-naked under the
showerheads, well, some hope, but as not a drop of water
comes out of the showerheads they give the handles another
turn, they're impatient, and then one of them is annoyed and
yells "This doesn't work!" and the one on the other side
shouts "Mine doesn't either," and everybody says, "Mine
neither, mine neither," are you getting the point, Dick? and
they go on like this until one of them, one who can smell a
little better, maybe because he never suffered from colds, or
polyps, or sinuses, yells, "The gas; this is a trap!" he yells,
understand? and then a terrific hubbub breaks out, Dick, and
first off, they all run toward the door, but it's hermetically
sealed and when they realize this they begin to punch each
other because they start to realize that dead men don't breathe
and those who don't breathe don't use up oxygen, and they
really go to it, Dick, you can hardly believe it, but heart and
soul, eh? and the weakest ones fall and the stronger ones,
Dick, kick them in their heads and their livers and their in-

testines and, as the air gets used up, the survivors (ten or so at first) throw themselves on the ones who've fallen (some ninety of them), just think how clever of them, Dick, and fasten their living lips on the dead lips and press down hard, just exactly like when you kiss a woman, like movie-theater kisses to be exact, and do mouth-to-mouth as hard as they can (not to give air but to take it) and suck up the air from the lifeless lungs, to the point, Dick, that the last survivor goes from one dead man to another (up to the ninety-ninth) one by one, greedily robbing them of the last breath that has stayed trapped in their alveoli and bronchial tubes and, finally, he says to himself with a last fleeting scrap of consciousness, "Have patience, Heinrich, others are worse off," are you getting the picture, Jacinto? and in those seconds of transition Heinrich also searches for the reference, that's logical, something to hold on to, and he thinks about the man who's walled up alive, I don't know where, in a niche or an alcove, tied hand and foot, that goes without saying, Heinrich, for as soon as a guy loses his lifesaving breasts he's threatened on every side, all right, well, he starts thinking about the man who's been walled up alive, two immense terrified eyes open to life above the gag (because he's gagged too, Heinrich, naturally) and with his two terrified eyes he watches the busy actions of the two masons and the apprentice, just imagine, one, two, three, four, five, six, seven, eight, nine, ten, eleven, twelve, thirteen, fourteen, fifteen, my fair lady! see, as masons have the habit of doing, brick by brick (putting them together with cement and smoothing the drips with the trowel), and the wall that's going to cut him off from the world grows higher and higher, but he (the man with the terrified eyes) can't do anything about it, Hein-

153

rich, because as I said he's tied good and tight, he can't even call them sons of bitches because, as I said, he's gagged, Heinrich, and so the wall keeps on rising and the space that's open to the light gets smaller and smaller, do you understand, Heinrich? and the man with the terrified eyes keeps saying to himself, "Three rows left," "Now two rows left," "Now just one row left," "Now three bricks left," "Now two bricks left," "Now just one brick left," and when things reach this point the man stands on tiptoe, see, he wants to fill his terrified eyes with life, he stands on tiptoe to look through the opening which is like a peephole open to the wide world and, at last, after the peephole has been closed and he's left alone and in the dark, he says to himself, "Patience, Pepe," (or "Patience, Ivan,") "others are worse off." Do you understand what I'm telling you, Jacinto? D'you get it? That's what the man who's walled up thinks, and the man who's gassed thinks of the man who's walled up, and the sailor who sinks to the bottom in the compartment of a cruiser thinks about the man who's gassed, and so it goes, because once a man loses his security breasts, he has to find a substitute, that's natural, for if a man can't find some consolation he's not really trying, and I'm telling you, Jacinto, because I haven't the slightest interest in deceiving you, and after all, your situation isn't desperate or anything like it, look at the sailor for instance, with the skin flayed off his fingers, he's one big bruise, his underpants are dirty and the six thousand meters of water, or however many they are, pressing against the portholes, and the plates, and the bulkheads, and the rivets and he (the sailor) asking himself, "Where will it burst in?" because it's certain that it will burst in, it can delay more or less time but in the end it will burst in, Jacinto, but, before

154

it bursts in, the sailor keeps on trembling and, if he's weak and his courage fails him, he'll unfasten a hammock and use its rope to hang himself without delay from the bars of the tables or the hook where he (the sailor) used to fasten the hammock ropes every night, d'you get it, it really must be tough, hard to swallow, but ordinarily a man drinks life right down to the dregs, Jacinto, that's common knowledge, don't say it isn't because it's perfectly obvious, and if a tooth hurts him (a man, that is) they take it out, and if a kidney fails they take it out, and if a leg is bothering him they saw it off, and if it's his heart that doesn't work, well, they change it, they take it out of another man, and if the other man isn't dead yet, well, look, so much the better, more chance of success, with a new heart or an old heart what I want is to see the sun come up tomorrow, that's the way we are, Jacinto, we cling to life like limpets, my God, you'd think the world consisted of handing out sugared almonds, well, well, there's no cure for that, dust we are, and the sailor, perfectly quiet, waiting for the porthole to burst, he knows full well it'll burst in the end, maybe the second one on the port side or maybe the fifth one on the starboard side, under the circumstances it makes no difference, the water will pour into the compartment like a torrent, just imagine, with the pressure of six kilometers of water, unheard-of, it comes in roaring, like in a hydraulic plant, taking over everything, and the sailor, though the compartment is large, feels the water, almost without transition, on the following parts of his body: his ankles, his legs, his knees, his thighs, his genitals, his abdomen, his belly button, his stomach, his nipples, his collarbones, his throat, his chin, and his mouth. And, Jacinto, when the salty taste reaches his lips the sailor gives a start and *begins to swim, calm as can be, that's logical, because he knows all too well that he can't go far, only hold himself up in the water, but the water level rises rapidly, while the ceiling line (made of metal plates scrupulously riveted in the shipyard) stays unchanged, in its place, just put yourself in his shoes, the anguish, the poor sailor's anguish that is, Jacinto, knowing that the supplies of oxygen and livable space are getting less by the second, but even though he knows it he keeps swimming, Jacinto, now it's only obstinacy and clinging to life, don't say it's not, but he keeps swimming and since he's in the dark he can't see the waterline and the ceiling line gradually getting closer, until, thump, the top of his head hits, thump, on a rivet, and in that instant, though it may seem to you, Jacinto, that there's nothing more terrible in the world, the sailor tells himself, "Patience, Dick, others are worse off," and he thinks of the gassed victims or the man walled up alive, but the water, no matter how much he thinks about it, doesn't stop, it goes on rising, you understand? and when it (the water) reaches his nose he (the sailor) keeps on swimming, putting his head a little to one side so that the water won't get into his mouth and nose and though it can be said that everything's over, he (the sailor) still holds out, presses his right ear against the steel plate, presses hard, and even though the space with oxygen in it is very small, he presses it harder and harder, and then, Jacinto, he turns around, so that his nose is the only thing that sticks out of the water, but since its level keeps on rising, the sailor crushes his nostrils against the plates of the ceiling, presses harder, using more and more force, until his nasal bones crack and the cartilage is smashed and begins to bleed (he notices it, of course, because the liquid around his nasal cavity is warm*

156

now), but he keeps on pressing, Jacinto, hear me? he presses with all his heart and soul and maybe he prays, maybe he curses, maybe he curses the mother who bore all wars, maybe he thinks about his wife or his child and, all of a sudden, just as he hears the creak of a watertight door bursting, the two lines (the waterline and the ceiling line) come together, imagine how horrible, just thinking about it drives you crazy, and the sailor strikes his head against the plates (as if it were possible to undo with your head the rivets so conscientiously tightened in the shipyard) until at last, half-asphyxiated, he gives up and even though the darkness is very profound he (the sailor) senses, or sees, a line of bubbles ever farther apart over his head, the images of his wife or child are blotted out and he feels as if someone has put a five-hundred-ton boulder on his chest and he (the sailor, of course) tries in vain to roll it off and, as he does so, he tears off his buttons, rips open his gray fatigues, his fingers contract (with wrinkled fingertips like Señorita Josefita's, Jacinto), his mouth opens, his eyes pop, his right leg jerks up and down spasmodically four or five times and, finally, he stops moving and his body slides softly down (as the cruiser had done before) until it rests (in the prone position) on the linoleum of the floor, on top of the grooves where he used to set up the tables every day. Now look here, Jacinto, how are you going to compare your fate with the fate of that guy, tell me that, you bundle of nerves? And then, who knows, maybe some fine day a diver finds the sunken ship and takes the notion to search for unimaginable treasures there, and that skeleton (the sailor's), on which the fish haven't left a miserable scrap of skin, means nothing to him, Jacinto, or at most he'll think, "Another man who died in the disaster," but he thinks it just with his mouth (or his head), Jacinto, without feeling it, because for a man who's searching for treasure the word disaster doesn't mean disaster, that goes without saying, Jacinto, I don't know whether I'm making myself clear or not, because for him (the diver), who's after a treasure, dead men don't count and disasters aren't disasters but possibilities. That's what life is like, Jacinto, don't kid yourself, and if you think about it a little bit you'll realize that your situation isn't bad enough to get desperate about, there are worse things, of course there are, the trouble with you is you're a kind of a nervous type, when, really, what has to be done here has got to be done with your head, Jacinto, nerves are what you've got too much of, you can be sure of that, cunning is better than strength, for you to start digging a tunnel ten meters long is a crazy job, I'll say, ten meters inch by inch, you're not in your right mind, Jacinto, fine hands you have, and great knotty biceps (Jeez, look what a bump Susanita just raised!), come on, now, what do you expect them to be like, you haven't taken a break for I don't know how long, Jacinto, you don't eat or rest, under those conditions anything could happen to you, a case of flu, for instance, will catch you with your defenses down and carry you off before you have time to think.

He (Jacinto) regards himself mutely, intensely, in the mirror and mentally deplores the way he looks: the exhausted, bitter grimace at the corners of his lips; the straggling beard growing in clumps; the purplish bags under his eyes; the dilated, expressionless pupils; the white head; the waxen pallor of the skin; the trembling hands . . . He shakes his head in protest and muses, "Keep calm, Jacinto; others are worse off."

As he emerges from the toilet (gentlemen) he sees the

calendar: MAY. "What day in May?" he asks himself. And he examines the red and black numbers and tells himself, by way of orientation, "We started out on May 5." He (Jacinto) tries hard to lay hands on a clue, to recall events, to arrange them chronologically, he resorts to the hedge, to the treecreeper's nest, the sun, the moon, and, suddenly inspired, runs for the transistor radio, turns it on, click, but, after he has turned it on, the silence grows deeper. "The batteries," he (Jacinto) says to himself. "The batteries are damp." He turns the transistor on and off a dozen times, click-click, click-click, click-click, shakes it (the transistor), but the transistor is like an open but silent mouth, like the mouths of the ninety-nine gassed victims after the last survivor has sucked the air out of their lungs. Jacinto feels an itch in his hand, a burning desire to smash it (the transistor) against the wall, but finally he restrains himself and tells himself to be calm: "What has to be done here has got to be done with your head," he tells himself.

Standing in front of the calendar again, going over the numbers from 6 to 31, he (Jacinto) hopes that a light or some other magic signal will, unexpectedly, reveal the day he is living in. And, as he passes the 10, he notices a sort of uneasiness in his stomach, but ignores this symptom and tells himself, "It's not possible. I've been here more than four days. That's not the signal," he tells himself,but the uneasiness grows as he pauses on the 20, and when he reaches the 30, his nausea is so severe that he has to go out into the open air to keep from vomiting. Outside, in a cold sweat, bent over at the waist beside the hedge, he (Jacinto) thinks, "It's that damned zero," and, though he is assailed by three violent spells of retching, he brings up only a bit of yellowish liquid.

As he straightens up, the first thing Jacinto sees is the rectangular hole, the heaps of porous earth piled on its edges. And the guy with the spade comma with his long thick mustache spattered with dirt comma asked what about the head, are you going to bury it without the head? comma he asked comma and the woman looked sidewise at Darío Esteban comma put her handkerchief to the corner of her right eye and said comma do it like that, don't worry about the head period Darío Esteban stood there dignified and distant comma next to the woman comma stuffed into the dark overcoat he wears for special occasions comma hatless comma his felt hat in his plump gloved hands comma folded flaccidly over his belly comma his shoetips apart comma his head respectfully bowed in the direction of the hole parenthesis as when one tries to demonstrate a funerary interest greater than what one really feels close parenthesis comma and the guy with the mustache carefully filled the shovel and when the earth fell on earth it produced a compatible noise comma plink comma a noise that was even harmonious comma but when it fell on the headless body it rumbled booom comma it sounded hollow and the guy with the shovel explained comma the stinker's fuller of air than a drum comma and the woman with the handkerchief sighed and Jacinto saw the earth encrusted in the beautiful thick hair of the back comma which was covered after three shovelfuls comma in such a macabre way that the decapitated body emerged from the ground at both ends colon at one end the neck comma the clean cut at the neck with the tubes of the esophagus and the trachea and at the other end comma the hindquarters comma the last brown spots on the whitish fur comma the hairy protuberance of the coccyx over the anus comma and the backward-bent stiffened joints of the legs period In a few minutes the hole was filled and the guy with the mustache comma with exquisite care comma scratched away raack-raack with the tip of the shovel at the rest of the turned earth and artistically formed a kind of heap or mound on the grave period When he finished comma Darío Esteban cleared his throat and the woman sighed again and Jacinto San José comma to break the tension comma leaned toward the woman and told her comma whenever they dig a hole there's dirt left over when they close it and the woman sighed and wiped her bloodshot eyes with her handkerchief and Darío Esteban said semicolon what Jacinto San José says is true; I don't know what causes it but every time they dig a hole there's dirt left over and Jacinto shrugged his shoulders and the woman sighed and Darío Esteban cleared his throat tritely comma while his gloved hand disappeared momentarily under his charcoal gray overcoat to reappear with a folded paper which he held out to the woman and the woman comma before she took it comma grabbed the lower part of her coat with both hands and made a sort of bow and comma then comma took the paper comma hid it in her bosom and said comma after taking in the grave with a distrustful glance comma may God repay you, Darío Esteban comma and Darío Esteban cleared his throat tritely again and said half a million, you will observe that Don Abdón has considered his death as in line of duty and has paid off as if your husband had been on the payroll since his demotion. I understand that the Company could not have been more generous. Dear lady, I share your grief end of paragraph

The guy with the shovel comma leaning on its handle comma looked on at all this comma and Jacinto's blue comma immaculate eyes looked on at all this and suddenly comma the woman knelt comma took Darío Esteban's hand between her two hands and kissed it several times with smacking kisses and comma although Darío Esteban tried to get away from the woman comma she kept it up comma she even wiped her eyes and her nose with his hand comma and kept saying all the time blessings on you and Don Abdón that's the way to take pity on the poor and comma as soon as he could comma Darío Esteban made his escape and took refuge in the cherry-colored car and Serafín started it parenthesis the car close parenthesis comma but the woman kept on yelling may God reward you, Darío Esteban and here is a humble servant who will do anything either of you want to ask comma and Darío Esteban smiled and waved goodbye with two gloved fingers and smiled nodding behind the back window of the car end of paragraph

He (Jacinto) lifts his head and sees the moist red earth piled on the edges of the hole. The nausea has left him (Jacinto) though his stomach still feels uncomfortable. "Keep calm," he tells himself, "what has to be done here has got to be done with your head," "Head," he repeats automatically and, without thinking about it further, goes into the hut, stoops down, searches under the bookcase, picks up the glass eye and the ruined antelope's head, throws the ruined antelope's head and the glass eye into the hole and shoves the piles of red earth with his feet, plop-plop, until they are buried. He breathes in deeply and exhales the air in whistles, wheee-wheee, intermittently, enjoying them, as if he were making music. He (Jacinto) repeats this controlled breathing several times, and finally he opens his arms wide and does the exercise for double pectorals, though his biceps and armpits hurt with every movement he makes. He stops doing it (the gymnastic exercise) and tells himself, "The question hinges on opening a passageway," and he starts to think about fire again as the most active and consistent element but he (Jacinto) delivers himself the following warning: "You've got to gamble everything on a single card. Lots of little efforts aren't going to get us anywhere," he says and, immediately, seizes the axe and begins to chop up the furniture (tables, bench, chairs, sofa, armchairs, stools, night table, chest of drawers, bed) and the decorations (pictures, drapes, curtains, books, railings, shutters, and the split logs and paneling from both inside and outside the house). When he has finished he piles the pieces of furnishings on the hedge, pushing them well inside it and, tossing some of them on top, sprinkles them with gasoline from the last container and sets fire to them. Under the blazing sun, the flames are almost invisible, but the crackling of the green sprouts, crrip-crrip, the frantic crepitation, crack-crack, allow him (Jacinto) to imagine the violence of the fire, and, on the other hand, when he sees how the metallic-looking leaves, and the bulbs, and the buds, and the stems shrivel and change their green color for brown and

curl up and sway back and forth, finally, dead, he is convinced of its efficacy. As the minutes go by the combustion does not slacken (or weaken) and Jacinto smilingly
watches the devastating progress of the bonfire, the
charred cavity (growing ever larger), the runners and
stems, first incandescent, then scorched, falling to the
ground like reeds, and he smiles, but with his habitual
pessimism, he tells himself that he should have adopted
this desperate measure several days ago. If the wind
blows (from the west), the smoke descends and becomes
so thick that Jacinto can hardly breathe and covers his
nose with a handkerchief while the birds on the front
and sides of the hedge fly up with a shrill whistle of
alarm, pi-piiic. There are blackbirds, thrushes, redwings, sparrows, treecreepers, grosbeaks, warblers,
finches, goldfinches, nightingales, robin redbreasts and,
in general, thicket birds, and all of them make a great
noise (each louder than the others) with their wingbeats,
whirr-whirr-whirr, and their whistling, bic-piiic-twitt,
and Jacinto is sad when he imagines the destroyed nests
the birds will refuse to go back to and this thought depresses him and once more he tells himself, "One side
can't win unless the other side loses" (pure mercantil-
ism), and yet Jacinto (who realizes that perversity is beginning to take him over and recognizes that he is
selfish, blind, and culpable) smiles at the fire and
destruction because only the fire and destruction can free
him, so he smiles at the fire and destruction, though the
birds and plants must die, but when he thinks that the
hedge could just as well be his begonia, his sansevieria,
and his ficus (watering plants is a job for young ladies,

164

Master Jacinto), he has to shut his eyes even though his lips continue to smile and his smile is interrupted only when the crackling subsides and then he opens his eyes and observes that the fire is dying down, the crackling noises come less often and soon, amid the smoke, his (Jacinto's) irritated eyes see a big cavity, but he waits a few more minutes until the flames have gone out and there is nothing left, in the charred hollow, but some live embers on a smoking bed of ash. He (Jacinto) hasn't the patience to wait for the embers to turn to cinders and decides to pour water on them, but as he starts around to the back of the hut he sees with stupefaction that the hedge is in the way, it blocks his progress, has joined on to the house; the new growth, the branches, the offshoots, have fastened their harmless-looking little stingers to the wall (from its base to the roof) and their runners have established themselves between the logs and the stones, are climbing along them and spreading out in all directions, some upward, smothering the eaves and snaking along the slate roof, and others are growing sidewise, curling around the split logs of the outer walls, leaping from one to another, progressing incessantly. In view of this obstacle, Jacinto goes through the house and emerges behind it by way of the kitchen window, screws the hose onto the kitchen faucet and returns once more, crossing the cabin, holding the other end of the hose with his index finger (against the growing water pressure) and, once on the threshold, aims it at the embers and listens delightedly to the hissing, sssssst, made by the cold water on the incandescent embers and watches, with a faint feeling of hope, the thick cloud of black smoke that de-

165

taches itself from the interrupted flames, but as the smoke disperses his (Jacinto's) hope also diminishes. The charred area has a radius of perhaps three meters, but sticking out of the ground are vigorous scorched stumps which, even in case they would permit access to the gate, would keep it from swinging freely. Jacinto runs into the charred area even though his shoes give off a suffocating stink of burned rubber, and among the burned branches and tobacco-colored leaves, he finds the remains of the gate.

The fire has devoured it (the gate) too, and yet the stems and branches keep him from reaching the place where it was located. Instantly Jacinto regrets what he has done, deplores having eliminated the boards of the benches and the bed, the paneling and log facing from inside and outside, which, if properly lashed together, like a raft, could, perhaps, have served to make a bridge over the hedge and recover his freedom. His (Jacinto's) heart pounds in his chest, tick-tack, tick-tack, in a quicker rhythm. He crosses the cabin again and clambers up to the roof by way of the wellhead. The spectacle from the roof is discouraging and the mere fact of looking at the bottom of the valley crossed by the brook with its transparent water, the fallow field with its turned earth, the reddish tussocks next to the abandoned millstones, the group of beehives, the slopes sprinkled with young oak trees (which are just beginning to show their summer leaves) and the vultures taking off solemnly (surely because of him) from the boulders across the valley, all this makes him (Jacinto) feel an uncomfortable empty place in the pit of his stomach, an empty feeling which turns to anguish when he sees how insignficant is the charred area in the total volume of the hedge: "Like the hole a nail makes in a wall," Jacinto thinks, graphically, and, suddenly, he is absorbed by the moving presence of the boldest stems crawling along the slate shingles and feels, as he watches them, a cold fear, which turns him to stone, as if he were surrounded by poisonous snakes and, taking care not to slip, he returns to the hut by way of the well, repeating mechanically, "You're shipwrecked, you're shipwrecked, you're shipwrecked," and under the influence of this obsessive idea he (Jacinto) goes into the cabin, takes some sheets of paper and a ballpoint pen and, using the hearth for the purpose, writes a dozen and a half times: I'M A PRISONER OF THE HEDGE. URGENTLY NOTIFY DON ABDON, LTD. THANKS. JACINTO SAN JOSE. Then he rolls up the pieces of paper one by one and, one by one, puts them into the empty alcohol and wine bottles and when these run out he goes to the cellar, takes nine (bottles), empties them out, lets them drain thoroughly, and hides away the remaining messages in them. Then he goes out to the tiny rectangle he has cleared and tosses bottle after bottle up over the hedge, but despite the fact that Jacinto throws them properly, that is, seizing them by the neck so as to give them more force, he is discouraged as he hears the vegetal impacts, plop-plop, the soft, padded noise produced by the foliage as it receives and devours the bottles. In the face of this new disappointment, Jacinto decides to climb up on the roof to throw them from a greater height, even choosing beforehand the place where he wants them to land, but the first bottle that falls beyond the hedge hits a stone and bursts into a thousand splinters, clink! After several attempts, Jacinto is successful with a patch of groundberry which softens the impact and the bottle rolls down the slope until he (Jacinto) loses sight of it. "It's useless," he says to himself suddenly; "if anyone should discover the bottles, he would also discover this monstrous hedge and would hear me yelling," Jacinto tells himself.

The sun striking the window of the cabin, though it is in shadow, reflects his dejected image and Jacinto takes advantage of this to speak frankly to himself, *because you're sunk in the most total and absolute impotence, don't kid yourself, my boy, let's be realists, we'll get nowhere by not calling things by their names, and if you yell it's going to be the same as if you whistle, just one more noise, because if the world is deaf there's no use shouting, and if the world is blind nobody can read your messages, Jacinto, it's better for you to get used to the idea from the beginning and start to live in reality. The world doesn't see, or hear, or understand, because the blind don't see and the deaf don't hear and nobody can understand what he doesn't see or hear, Jacinto, that goes without saying, you've been abandoned and your situata, you see I'm speaking to you with franka, is despera and the only consolata in these circums is the convicta that a vegeta strangleho is more tolera and accepta than a minera or anima one. Others are worse off Jazo, just look at the sailo in a cruis sent to the botto by an enem torpo, all alo, in a comparta, and the saltwa pouring in the portho, get it? and the water leve going up and up: for starts, the anks, then the legs, the kneejoins, the thighs, the testis, the abdo, the bellybun, the stoma, the nipps (Don Abdón's swelling breasts,*

*with black nourishing nipples, could maybe be a refuge for
his misfortune), the collarbos, the chin, the cheeks, the mouth
. . . That's worse, a thousand times worse, no matter how
you look at it, don't try to kid me, Jazo, and the situata of a
gasvicti or a wallshut man, I'll say, enough to make you lose
your marbs, but losing his head is a luxury only Gen can
allow himself, Jacinto, you know that, losing it and getting
it stuffed, but you, you, in these circumstances, have to keep
it on your shoulders, d'you hear? and good and tight too,
because problems do get solved, but not with nerves, or hys-
terics, I'm telling you so you'll catch on, but by thinking it
out, and if you can't go out by the door, as you came in, or
underneath, digging a tunnel, like the rabbits, well, look, the
only chance you've got to go up, d'you hear? like the birds.*

"Birds," he (Jacinto) repeats, and his glance slides upward, up the windowpane, up the logs, up the eaves to
the blue of the sky, where the vultures are slowly wheeling (and underneath them a smaller vulture), flying above
the ravine. "Like the roc in the *Thousand and One Nights*,"
he (Jacinto) says to himself and recalls the soft lap of his
early childhood years, the life saving breasts, the invulnerable security teats, against which his little body was
pressed softly, progressively, sweetly, until the last drop
of suspiciousness or fear escaped from it (from his little
body). Jacinto's eyes are suffused with nostalgia. "There's
nothing left of that," he says to himself and, immediately, comes back to reality and repeats "birds," and immediately, his imagination is unleashed and, immediately, he (Jacinto) goes into action, fetches from the cabin
a ball of twine (hemp, the toughest kind on the market)
and cuts ten pieces of two meters each, makes slipknots

169

in the ends of each one, lies on the ground with two of them in each hand and pretends he's dead. In this position, the sun is hotter and Jacinto enjoys relaxing, feeling the vertical rays falling on his exhausted body. With extreme caution, he opens his eyelids from time to time and again and again observes with discouragement that the vultures have not changed position, they continue their lazy wheeling, very high, gliding as if they were flying without effort. "This is an old wives' tale," he (Jacinto) says to himself at last. "Vultures don't come down to dead bodies because they're lying down but because they stink," he says, and sits down on the stones, throws the strings away, and watches the strip of blue sky, growing ever narrower, which shows between the two lateral strips of hedge. The best-developed of the plant tips, whose height is that of two men (one on the shoulders of the other), are visibly arching toward each other, seeking each other out, as if mutually attracted to one another, so it is easy to see that in two or three days they will join and form a tunnel over his head and, when that happens, the possibilities of escape will have vanished. He hears a convulsive rush of wings over his head, swish-swish-swish, and sees a woodpigeon rapidly cross the open space. "A pigeon," he tells himself ingenuously, "I thought it was a vulture." He jumps up without ceasing to stare at the hedge's thick branches: "Within six days they will have asphyxiated me," he thinks. Another pigeon crosses fleetingly over his head and, at once, he thinks, "Pigeons, carrier pigeons, messenger pigeos, messer pigeos. That's it!" he yells suddenly. "A carrier pigeon!" His whole body trembles with excitement. "The problem is to trap them," he says to himself. "How do you catch a bird?" He remembers his evening walks along the esplanade beside the lake, the slow crumbling of the loaf of bread, with the pigeons, roor-r-r, and the sparrows, cheep-chissis, perched on his head, his forearms, and his shoulders. "They're my friends," he (Jacinto) smiles and hastily grabs a container of bread, tears off the plastic that preserves it from dampness and crumbles it into a heap. Then he sprinkles the crumbs all over himself, on his head, his shoulders and his left arm, squats with the greatest care so that the crumbs won't fall off, takes a handful of them (the crumbs) with his right hand, and places himself with the greatest care in the most visible part of the rectangle that hasn't yet been invaded by plant growth, stretches out his arms, his heels together, and settles down, waiting patiently for the birds to descend. Out of the corner of his eye he watches two sparrows, cheep-chissis, enjoying the leftover crumbs on the ground two meters away and Jacinto smiles to himself. "Now they're alighting," he thinks hopefully, and, indeed, after five minutes there are four sparrows and then six and soon there are twelve (sparrows), but after they have polished off the crumbs that are scattered on the stones they return to the foliage or the eaves and chirp. In view of their reluctance, Jacinto purses his lips and begins to whistle softly, whee-whoo-whee, varying the pitch, moving only the muscles strictly necessary to make the whistling noise, whee-whoo-whee, but the birds ignore the lure and his arms begin to feel heavy, but he (Jacinto) keeps on whistling, whee-whoo-whee, without changing the rhythm or

171

stress, until his arms feel like lead and, without realizing
that he is doing it, he gradually lowers them (his arms),
so that a few crumbs roll down the slope and fall on the
ground and scarcely have they touched the ground than
the sparrows (waiting alertly in the foliage and on the
eaves) hastily swoop down on them but not one has the
idea of flying up to his arms or shoulders and Jacinto
can't whistle any more because his lips have become
numb, but because the facial muscles haven't the strength
to expand, Jacinto squats there with his lips pursed, as
if he were about to kiss someone, until, finally, he gives
up, lets his arms fall dejectedly and the crumbs slide to
the ground and, instantly, a flock of sparrows, cheep-
chissis-cheep, surround him (Jacinto) and gobble them
(the crumbs) up in a wink.

While he was waiting, Jacinto has remembered one of
his conversations with César Fuentes (nicknamed Cesarina) on the riverbank, on the sunny spring afternoons
when he (Jacinto) was trying to bring him (César Fuentes)
out of his deep depression. César Fuentes, like all small-
town youngsters, knew the tricks of the expert bird-
catcher: the net, the baits, the snare at the edge of ponds,
traps made with a nut and a washbasin, and, finally, the
perfidious nocturnal procedure of dazzling them with a
lantern as they sleep. Jacinto mentally rejects the first
three lures (net, bait, and snare), thinks again and remembers that in the cupboard, among the stores of food,
there is a big bag of walnuts. He goes there, grabs a
handful and carefully makes holes in them (the secret of
this trick lies in the fact that the bird must peck precisely
in the prepared hole) and, to substitute for the basin

172

(which he can't find), Jacinto decides to use the biggest saucepans and cooking pots. Now Jacinto recalls the stratagem in all its details. One by one he balances the pots over the nuts, their (the nuts') hole toward the inside of the pans, so that the bird will have to slip under it (the pan) if it wants to peck at the kernel, so that with each peck at a kernel the pan's balance becomes more uncertain, and finally, the rim of the pan slips over the curve of the nut and traps the bird inside it (the pan). So he (Jacinto) sets up the traps, leaving a space of one meter between them, goes into the cabin and takes up his post at the front window. Hidden behind the slats of the blind, Jacinto has a perfect view of the six devices. As soon as Jacinto enters the house, the sparrows return to the paving stones and hop around among the blocks, looking for breadcrumbs in the cracks and among the spears of grass that grow between them and each time that one of the birds comes close to a saucepan or a pot, or simply looks with its suspicious brown eye at a saucepan or a pot, Jacinto's breath chokes in his throat. He isn't thinking about eventual success but of the fact that at the moment he has made of the game (of trapping a bird) a question of life or death. But the sparrows don't seem to be interested in the nuts and yet, when he (Jacinto) least expects it, the pot nearest the hedge falls down, plop-boom, on the stones and he (Jacinto) presses his eye against the slats of the blind and sees near the edge of the pot the tip of a creeping shoot. Jacinto's mouth dries up and his stomach contracts: "My God!" he says. "Within two days they'll eat me up!" but the buzzard which has just landed on the paving stones after describing a graceful semicircle, distracts him (Jacinto), taking all his attention. The buzzard, as soon as it has taken in the situation, heads in a series of small hops for the second nut on the left. Jacinto trembles and instinctively moves one hand (invisible to the bird) as if encouraging it (the buzzard) toward the pot, while with the other (hand) he unbuttons his shirt. Emotion chokes him, but the bird is suspicious of the pot and, once near the nut, administers three blows with its beak on the shell (that is, from the outside in), so ferociously that the nut rolls and the pot falls, plop-boom, and traps the nut while the buzzard flies up, startled, and lights on a creeper, from which vantage point it analyzes the situation with an alert glance from its eyes. It moves its head from side to side as if trying to convince itself that nobody is there, that all that battery of pans and pots isn't a snare, and after a while it returns to the charge, and now, its objective is the third nut on the right. At first the bird doesn't peck at it, but describes a semicircle, stops, regards the nut distrustfully, then looks at the door of the cabin, hesitates, describes another semicircle in the opposite direction (also counterclockwise), hesitates again and, finally, gives three hops and slips under the pot. Jacinto holds his breath, his nose pressed against the slats. He (Jacinto) doesn't even blink and twice he makes the motion of unbuttoning the top button of his shirt, which is already unbuttoned. The buzzard's tail, which sticks out from under the edge of the pot, flips up and down, disappears, and its head appears on the other side, that is, it comes out again. Jacinto becomes impatient, blames himself for his lack of skill, but, just then, the bird gives

174

four little hops and hides under the pot again. Its peck must have been so fierce that the pan wavers from side to side over the nut and the nut takes a forty-five-degree turn and, on the second peck, it (the nut) turns another forty-five degrees so that the hole that leaves the kernel exposed is visible. The buzzard gives a third peck outside the trap and when the nut rolls and the pan falls, plop-boom, the bird is startled and flies off for good over the hedge. Jacinto draws back from the blind muttering to himself, opens the door, picks up a stone, sits on the bench outside the door and begins to crack nuts, crack-crack-crack, and eat them as he muses, "There's nothing to do but wait for nightfall."

Before it becomes completely dark, as soon as the sun has set behind the mountain and the flowers begin to give off their sweet, sticky odor, Jacinto takes refuge in the cabin and adopts the following precautions: he lowers the blinds (previously unrolling the cord when they are halfway down so that the blinds will fall all at once, ra-ta-bla, and won't leave cracks between them; locks the sash windows; fills to the top the storage well of the portable lamp and dresses in black shoes, black pants, and navy-blue sweater and shirt. "It's the last chance," he thinks. "I can't make any mistakes." For some time now the birds have been quiet after their sunset chirping (twi-twi, check-check, sib-sab, teet-teet). Not a sound can be heard. Jacinto sets the lamp on the stove and strides nervously from the door to the bed, from the bed to the door. His shadow, cut in two at the point where the wall meets the floor, is also black and sinister. The effect is strange, Jacinto in his dark clothing walking up and down that stripped empty room (with the exception of the bed). He (Jacinto) doesn't know exactly what he's waiting for but, as soon as he hears the woody cry of the nightjar (quick-quick-quick) on the road, Jacinto picks up the lamp and leaves the hut. The odor of the hedge is so intense that he can hardly endure it, but, convinced of the need to carry out his project, he approaches it (the hedge), holding the lamp in front of him, and opens the foliage with the other hand (the one that isn't holding the lamp). The breasts of two wrens in flight gleam whitely in the air, tit-tit-tit, like two flashes. Jacinto tries to act with as much caution as possible, and, at first sight, it seems to him that the hedge is empty (despite his conviction that it has hundreds of inhabitants) but, as he looks more closely, he discovers the small palpitating breast of a robin among the tangled leaves, its little round, sleepy eyes hypnotized by the light, so that Jacinto has only to stretch out his hand and catch it. When he feels in his hand the bird's struggles, its frantic beating, its anguished tsissips, Jacinto's eyes soften and he almost cries out for joy. "I won't hurt you," he murmurs. He is moved by that warm littleness, the sensation of a live body in contact with his orphan skin. "I won't hurt you," he whispers to it and delicately places the bird in his pants pocket. The robin's tiny restless movements next to his (Jacinto's) abdomen make him feel tender. Without moving from the spot and within a few seconds, Jacinto's eyes (now accustomed to the darkness) spy two treecreepers (on the nest) and a crested warbler. Jacinto hesitates over the treecreepers, but the flame of malignity which has surfaced at other times during his

176

confinement gets the better of him, he puts out his hand and grabs them (the treecreepers) without any hesitation. In the still-warm nest four little spotted eggs, whose image pursues him for several minutes, shine whitely. He (Jacinto) soon forgets them, he is metamorphosed into a hunting beast, with his luminous eye and his insatiable claws. Now he can see sleeping birds, in confusion, everywhere. And he catches them and puts them in his pockets, catches them and puts them in his pockets, with the activity of a boy stealing hazelnuts. The bumps in his pockets stir and communicate to his (Jacinto's) astonished abdomen an ambiguous, maternal palpitation. From time to time, a frog croaks down below, co-ac-co-ac, in some backwater of the river. Jacinto smiles happily. At more or less long intervals he enters the cabin and, after closing the door, empties his pockets of birds which, stupefied, flit around him and around the lamp, describing bats' circles and parabolas, cheeping and chirping wildly, to eventually take refuge in dark corners or settle on the metal skeleton of the bookcase. By the time he has finished his search of the front hedge, Jacinto estimates that he has caught approximately a hundred birds (he has been counting them but when some escaped from his pockets he lost count). Despite this, he keeps on searching, so that when he again takes refuge in the cabin after five hours, the noise of cheep-cheeps, bick-bicks, check-checks, is really deafening, but as far as Jacinto is concerned that untimely concert, the reckless flight all around him, stimulates him and makes his bloodless lips smile; and his blue eyes, which have been gloomy and introspective also smile, and the hairs

177

in his beard smile too, and his ears and the flare of his nostrils, everything in him (Jacinto) smiles as he sits down on the floor and starts to write on the hearth of the fireplace, on little pieces of paper, with his careful calligraphy, the dramatic message: "HELP! I'M A PRISONER OF HEDGE IN REST AND RECUPERATION HUT NO. 13. NOTIFY DON ABDON, LTD. JACINTO SAN JOSE."

When the first fifty messages are ready, Jacinto lays down the pen, takes a roll of adhesive tape and, one by one, starts catching birds (at each movement he makes, the dozens of shut-in birds go wild and some smash against the walls or the windowpanes and fall to the floor, dying), but he (Jacinto) pays no attention to the victims, now it does not move him in the least to find heaps of bodies if he can regain his freedom at their expense; he is like the last survivor of the gassed victims (he shakes his head violently to dispel this picture) and, one by one, he rolls his appeal for help around the birds' skinny little legs and then fastens it with a small piece of adhesive tape. The operation is a slow one, because for each messenger bird he prepares he has to open the door and let it out through a crack into the darkness of night. But Jacinto does not tire of the task, he does not feel the slightest fatigue, perhaps because with each bird that he frees it seems to him as if he were freeing part of himself. And just as the blinds let the bright light of dawn filter in, Jacinto finishes rolling up the last messages, looses the last prisoner (a redwing), sighs deeply, and walks toward the cot dragging his feet and, without taking off his black shoes or his dark clothes, falls into it (the cot), groans once, wheww!, groans again, wheww!, and falls deeply asleep.

When he awakes, he is overwhelmed by the feeling that he has slept for forty-eight hours or, perhaps, forty-eight days. He (Jacinto) can't be sure about it, but this has been his first restorative sleep in a long time and for a long time, that is, a prolonged sleep. The idea buzzes around vaguely in his confused head that there are reasons for satisfaction, but it is some time before he (Jacinto) remembers the messenger birds. He tries to open the blind at the head of the bed, but this time the slats do not obey his tug on the cord and its end lies motionless in his hand. Jacinto raises his eyes, disconcerted by this, and observes that some very thin stems, like creepers, are coming in through the cracks between the slats, and once they have overcome this obstacle, are beginning to twine together. And others are sprouting in the tiny space that separates the blind from the glass (one of the few windowpanes that are still intact). "They've blockaded it (the blind)," thinks Jacinto, and runs to the door which he manages to open after overcoming a stubborn resistance. The hedge frames the door like a climbing plant and the edges of the two strips of hedge have joined, forming an arch over the meter-wide space between them which barely lets the daylight in. Only from the threshold can he still see a bit of clear sky in which half a dozen vultures are flying. He does not see the sun, but guesses from the position and length of the shadows that it is late in the afternoon (of what day?) "Maybe six or seven in the evening" (thinks Jacinto). He nervously

179

rubs one hand against the other and at the sound, sss-sss-sss, a warbler flies up, check-check-check, and Jacinto smiles to himself: it has a little white bandage on its lower right leg. Jacinto throws a stone at the hedge and more birds fly out: blackbirds, finches, treecreepers, flycatchers . . . The same kinds as always. Astonished, he (Jacinto) discovers something that is half comforting, half disappointing: two out of every three birds have a white bandage on their lower right legs. Nervously, he (Jacinto) plunges into the vegetal tunnel clapping his hands, clap-clap-clap (the noise resounds like explosions), which startle birds on every side, confused birds who flit about in the small space and then settle again on the most visible branches: three out of every four birds have a white bandage on their right legs. Jacinto returns through the tunnel without ceasing to clap his hands (he finds in this action an exhausting method of letting off steam) and when he reaches the open space he sees the eaves and the fringes of the hedge and the tangled growth completely covered with birds (perhaps a hundred), all with a white bandage on their right legs. When he sees this spectacle he (Jacinto) loses his head, turns around clapping his hands ever more loudly, clap-clap-clap! kicks the lower parts of the hedge, thump-thump, and the birds (their right legs white) flit around and perch again and Jacinto yells, "You're great messenger birds, you are!" and "Lazy good-for-nothings!", that's what Jacinto yells, and the ravine says, respectively, "are" and "ings" and Jacinto, when he hears the ravine's answers, gets really mad, loses his temper and screams, "Do your duty, you rascals!" and the ravine answers "cals" and Jacinto, enraged, shouts, "Take my message out there!" and the ravine answers "ere" and Jacinto gets madder and madder and every time he sees a bird (which is constantly) with a white leg, he is beside himself, calls it all sorts of sweet nothings, threatens it with his clenched fist, until in one of these paroxysms he fetches up against the silent, threatening hedge, and makes a half-turn and fetches up against the other, untouched plant wall, and then his fury turns on it (on the hedge) and he challenges it at the top of his voice, "You can't beat me!" and the ravine says "me" and then he says "No!" and the ravine answers "no," and Jacinto adds, "Even if I have to shut myself in the cabin for three months!" and the ravine repeats "onths."

He (Jacinto) is shaking like a leaf, he can't stay quiet, his hair is beginning to curl, his yellow beard shining with sweat, his blue eyes wild; he (Jacinto) turns round and round, spins around three times and everywhere he collides with the dark hedge stretching out its tentacles, and when he raises his eyes, he sees it (the hedge) climbing (literally snaking its way) over the roof of the hut, curling around the corbels, the gutters, and the chimney, enwrapping everything wrappable. The yellow flowers, with their dusty stamens, are opening everywhere with short explosions, pop-pop-pop, and the stalks and new branches divide in two before his (Jacinto's) astonished eyes, and the new branches give birth to new bulbs (dark and swollen), and, if Jacinto watches them for a little while, he can witness their mute explosion. The hedge's proliferation is fabulous and progressive, that is, the larger it becomes the more rapid is its prop-

181

agation, and with its propagation its avid agressiveness increases.

Jacinto is so terrified that he doesn't know what to do. His head isn't working properly but he is conscious of one fact: by the next day he won't be able to open the door. In view of this contingency he twitches, clenches his fists, and yells, "No!" and "Damn them!" and the ravine answers "o" and "em," and when he hears the echo, he turns on the ravine (Jacinto needs a scapegoat) and, completely out of his head, carries on with it (the imperturbable ravine) the following dialogue:

"Damn you!"

"Oo!"

"Your mother's a . . ."

" 'S a . . ."

"Don't you insult her!"

"Her!"

"Fuck your mother!"

"Other!"

And there he stands (trembling at his own words), screaming and screaming, insulting and insulting, until he (Jacinto) falls to the ground in a fit of nerves, rolls over and over on the paving stones (like a baby donkey when it's frisking in a meadow), drooling, spitting out disconnected words, until, little by little, he becomes calmer and begins to utter short prayers aloud and, when he is in the middle of this, he sees through the open space where the sky is still visible, a pair of vultures, describing wide circles, flying much lower than a couple of hours ago. Jacinto watches them threateningly. "I won't give you that pleasure," he tells them, but by now his voice barely emerges from his body, he is completely hoarse and is soaked with sweat and, when he stands up and enters the hut, his legs feel weak at the knees and he walks haltingly, lurching from side to side, like an inexperienced sailor.

There is still light outside, but since the blinds are held fast, Jacinto leaves the door ajar and lights the kerosene lamp with which he takes a look at the cupboard and goes down to the cellar to take inventory of the food supplies. "On that score I can withstand a siege of two months; they'll come looking for me before then," he tells himself, and goes upstairs again and bolts the door.

His hands are shaking and their tremors transmit themselves to the lamp, which gives off a clinking noise, tinkle-tinkle. In the toilet (gentlemen), while he pees, he looks at himself in the mirror and doesn't recognize himself, his hair and beard are white and curly, with a disconcerting density of hair, like tufts of wool. Jacinto fingers his beard (when he finishes peeing), takes a good look at himself and says in a trembling voice, *it's no good shouting, Jacinto, believe me, because the world is deaf and blind, Jacinto, nobody's listening, d'you hear?, nobody wants to find out about what's going on in here, because things you don't know about are the same as things that aren't happening. But I ask myself, Jacinto, where are the poor in spirit, the pure in heart, the merciful, the peacemakers, they that mourn, those who hunger and thirst after righteousness, if any of them are left? Where are they, Jacinto? Go on, tell me, I'm asking you please, you know it, Jacinto, don't act like that, I need to find one, I swear to you, it's no whim, you can see that yourself, because if in the next two days a*

pure-in-heart, a merciful, a peacemaker, someone who hun-
gers and thirsts after righteousness doesn't show up, Jacinto,
you're a goner, you tell me, or is it that you don't realize?
You're seeing it happen the same as me, it isn't something
I've invented, because things, no matter how you look at
them, couldn't be worse . . . Come on, Jacinto! please, tell
me where they are, even if there's only one, speak up, by all
you love the most, don't be like that, no matter how hard it
is, Jacinto, or is it that the pure in heart, the merciful, the
peacemakers, they that mourn, those who hunger and thirst
after righteousness, are all gone? Is that it, Jacinto? Speak
up, please, even though it's hard to say it, are the fierce in
heart, the merciless, the warriors, the torturers, the unright-
eous the ones who have taken over the world?

Jacinto is panting. He (Jacinto) is sweating. Jacinto is
trembling. He (Jacinto) is crying. Jacinto clutches the
sides of the washbowl convulsively. He (Jacinto) shudders when the first crackling noise, crick, sounds, and
then he leaves the toilet and from the threshold sees, in
the hinge of the window, over his bed, he sees the tip
of a greenish-yellow stem, flanked by two leaves, like
two wings; it (the stem) looks like a dragonfly. Fascinated, he goes toward it and pulls it out with a jerk. But
scarcely has he cut it off than the crackling noise is repeated, crick, overhead, on the wood of the paneled ceiling (the only paneling he hasn't touched), and he (Jacinto) raises his eyes and, between two tigerwood boards,
he sees the tip of another whitish-green stem peeping
timidly through. From that moment on, the crackling
noises, crick-crick-crick, and the light impact of pieces of
plaster, pop-pop-pop, falling on the floor, are repeated

184

at very short intervals. They are cracklings, crick-crick, and almost imperceptible little blows, pop-pop, but they make Jacinto tremble as if they were guns going off. Jacinto becomes more and more nervous. After the third crackle, crick, Jacinto moves to and fro, constantly changing direction (he sees black shadows everywhere), guided by the crackle, crick-crick, of the boards and the impacts, pop-pop, of the pieces of plaster on the floor. The hedge's voracious infiltration makes him think of a pursuing animal and his pruning efforts (in the spots where the infiltration is taking place) strike him as a puerile response (something like cutting the nail-tips off a fabulous monster). Despite this (the realization of his impotence), Jacinto does not rest, he paces to and fro, examines the ceiling and the walls, the flooring, the window frames, and the closures of the door. He knows that he is being besieged and gradually his confidence in the cabin's powers of resistance decreases. The hedge's prodigious exuberance is unstoppable; only by exercising constant vigilance can he hold out for a time. And so Jacinto, every time he hears a noise, conscientiously investigates the sector the noise is coming from until he finds the reason or until a new crackle, crick, dryer and more penetrating than the previous one, shifts his attention and makes him break off his original search. In a few hours he (Jacinto) has torn loose so many stems that his fingers hurt and he decides that, from now on, he will use the pruning shears. There is one detail that frightens him: the new sprout of the amputated stem is twice as vigorous as the previous one, and this makes him (Jacinto) conclude that in a very short time they (the stems) will be impervious to the shears. This idea obsesses and bewilders him and, very often, he observes a sort of falling-away in his insides, as when, in the transition from waking to sleeping, the mattress collapses (or seems to), generally if he has stayed up too late or drunk too much. Pop-pop, crick, pop, crick-crick, crick, a moment comes when Jacinto can no longer cope. The penetrating, persevering stems are hounding him and the hedge is trying to break in through the roof, the walls, the windows, with a maddening crepitating sound. He (Jacinto) runs to and fro, does the work of ten, drags the bed (the only piece of furniture he can climb on) from the living room to the bedroom, from one corner to another, to reach the ceiling. He (Jacinto) is like a doctor who in the instants immediately following a catastrophe, drawn by the groans of the injured, wants to attend to all the cries for help simultaneously but, unable to multiply himself, attends to no one. Bewildered, his (Jacinto's) brain wanders in a labyrinth of sterile circumlocutions. What's the matter with you, Jacinto San José? You don't look so good. I get dizzy when I write zeroes. It's very surprising, you aren't making zeroes but Os, hadn't you noticed? That is idle gossip, doctor, to which you should pay no attention. It wouldn't be out of curiosity to know what you're adding? King kinging it on the mountain, shooting rockets like a fountain. Why do you say stupid things, Jacinto San José? Talk about the catenaccio defense. D'you think that the catenaccio defense is destroying soccer as a spectacle? The fly isn't the bad part, Darío Esteban, but thinking about the fly, if you don't think about the fly it's as if the fly didn't exist, understand? The only chance we humans had, the Tower of Babel, we threw it away like fools. But can you imagine, my boy, a free man without a coin in his pocket? Don Abdón, you are the most motherly father of all fathers. Then, are you insinuating, Jacinto San José, that order is not freedom? Jack, jack, under every bed a whack! Is it true that there are times when you have to write more zeroes than others before you get dizzy? The hedge is the defense of the timid. But can't you see that you're fucking up my field? It's an American hybrid that proliferates in a very short time; biology has never before achieved such marvels. What's the matter with you, Jacinto San José? You don't look so good. Only a short time ago, your illness would have meant the end, but nowadays the Company foresees these contingencies, for in the new order man has ceased to be an instrument. You wouldn't be saying that out of curiosity to know what you're adding, Jacinto San José? Stop, daddy, please, I'm going to fall. Protected by the hedge, you will be able to think deeply. Then, what distinction do you make between the o in Jacinto and the zeroes you wrote at the top of the page? It's an American hybrid that proliferates in a very short time. And you hadn't noticed anything until today? We were nothing until he came; we owe everything to his initiative. Well, what the fuck, if old Gen hasn't eaten the country boy's things! The Company is yours and by bringing honor to the Company you bring honor on yourselves. Under water for a bit, Don Abdón! It doesn't seem possible in so few years. Prize for the young lady! Talking about sports is even healthier than practicing them. You're timid, aren't you?

Avoiding responsibility is the first step toward being happy. You're timid, aren't you? What's the matter with you, Jacinto San José? You don't look so good. The Company is in no way trying to make things difficult for you and is ready to consider that your husband died in line of duty. Please understand me, after letting him die like a dog, I can't bear to bury him like a dog. You're timid, aren't you? It's an American hybrid that proliferates in a very short time. I understand your feelings, dear lady, and, in a certain sense, I share them. One question, Darío Esteban, the head, will you give us that too? I say only one thing: if we're playing partners you ought to say so from the start; as I understand it, the option leaves no room for doubt. They aren't dollars, or Swiss francs, or kilowatt-hours, or blacks, or girls in nightgowns, but addends. Neithe rheto nor diale, Daro Esta, eve attem at comprensa through the spowo is a uto. What kind of a nest have you fallen from, Master Jacinto? Forgive me, I presume that I owe you an explanation; the patient, by instinct, barricades himself behind what he believes to be his personality, but this does not exist, it is a mere potentiality. What's the matter with you, Jacinto San José? You don't look so good. To relax and obtain from him . . . Why do you say stupid things, Jacinto San José? . . . a spontaneous reaction we must previously have emptied him. Jeez! Look what a bump Susanita just raised. What a beautiful pointer! Isn't it? Well I say that the catenaccio defense, well I say that the catenaccio defense, well I say that the catenaccio defense . . . What's the matter with you, Jacinto San José? You don't look so

188

good. It's only a petit-bourgeois practice. Don't forget: the hedge is the defense of the timid.

"Timid," says Jacinto as he climbs out of bed. He stares vaguely and his head swims in a sea of confusion. Apart from this, Jacinto presents a very complex syndrome just at this time: intense cold in head and extremities; tremor in the hands; pointless feelings of haste and absolute inability to wait; mental confusion; anxiety. Jacinto guesses that the end has come, he bends over, unscrews the little bottle of sugar-coated pink pills and swallows three at once. Right after that, he (Jacinto) sits on the bed. After a few minutes his skin becomes transparent, like glass, so that he can see his insides, his veins and arteries, his bones, just as in a detailed anatomical engraving. Simultaneously the stems (nine of them), now stripped of buds and leaves, weak and skinny as tendrils, start to move, seeking out the orifices of his body. Jacinto can do nothing: he merely observes, as if he were something alien to his own person. The first stem, slippery and flexible as a catheter, goes in through his anus. Jacinto can see its little greenish-white head, at once tender and voracious, progressing through his rectum. The second stem goes in (painlessly) through his penis, through the urethra. The other seven (stems), after climbing up his (Jacinto's) transparent body, encircle his head and insert themselves into the following orifices: one into his mouth, two into his ears, two into his nostrils, and one more (the last) into his eyes. Jacinto feels no physical discomfort but he does feel the cold slithering, the tendrils' tickling sensations in his body orifices and channels. Once inside his (Jacinto's) body the invading stems advance along the following routes:

The one that enters his anus penetrates the rectum (the channels are also transparent, like plastic tubing), zigzags through the large intestine, the small intestine, attains the duodenum and reaches the stomach, where it joins the head of the stem that came in through his mouth and which has reached there (the stomach) through the pharynx and the esophagus. However, this latter stem, as soon as it has entered the mouth, divides into two, and while one heads for the esophagus (as has been said), the other travels through the larynx and the trachea and, once there, divides into a bunch of threadlike stems which enter the bronchia and the air sacs, lodging in the lungs. The one (stem) that entered through the penis climbs up the urethra, takes a turn around the bladder, divides in its turn, and each stem-end winds up in a ureter, they climb the ureters, confront the renal spaces and enter the kidneys. The stems that went in through the ears, sharp as needles, perforate the eardrums, traverse the hammer, anvil, stapes, and stirrup bones and encyst in the inner ears. Those that entered through the nostrils immediately divide, and while one end joins the stem that is descending the pharynx, the other climbs to the eye through the tear duct. Finally, those that went in through the eyes, reinforced by those that are breaking out through the tear ducts, attack the cribiform plate, form tiny threads, slip into all its minute channels, and, once the cribiform plate is filled, divide into fringe-like bunches which invade the circumvolutions of the brain: hippocampus, fissure of Silvio, fissure of Rolando, thal-

amus, hypothalamus, etc. And when the vital centers of
the body and brain have been occupied (in a bloodless
and stealthy operation), the surge of sap begins, all the
little stems suddenly become much greener, swell, fill
with bulbs and buds, and Jacinto feels a constantly wors-
ening pain, sharper and more tearing at every instant,
until all the sprouts burst in a brutal explosion and, simultaneously, the ureters, the esophagus, the intestines,
the air sacs, the tear ducts, the cribiform plate, the lungs,
the urethra, the rectum, the trachea, and the cranial cavity all burst, and, with the splitting apart of all his vital
channels, Jacinto's body loses its transparency, becomes
opaque and gradually takes on a brownish-grayish, ashy
tone, his belly swells into an extraordinary curve, and
suddenly, as if by sleight of hand, a gigantic yellow
flower sprouts from his navel.

Jacinto's shriek, aaaaaah! is shattering, bloodcurdling;
he turns his head and opens his puffy eyes; from the
dampness of his cheek he deduces that while he was half
asleep he has drooled. He (Jacinto) sits up in bed, his
head in the grip of a painful torpor. He doesn't understand how he got there (in bed) with his dark clothes
and his black shoes on. He doesn't understand anything.
By the very small amount of light that comes in through
the blinds he recognizes the invasion that has taken place:
the vegetal stalactites, the climbing runners, the flowering shoots were breaking in everywhere. The pruning
shears are there (he doesn't know why either) in the hollow his bottom forms in the mattress, and he picks them
(the pruning shears) up and as if, after long reflection,
he has decided to get rid of someone, he stands up with

them (the pruning shears) held high, and furiously attacks the branches that are coming in through the cracks of the door and the windows, that hang from the ceiling, that creep along the walls and the floor, crick-crack, boldly. The clicking of the shears, crick-crack, momentarily appeases him (Jacinto). He tries to cut very short, right down to the surface either of the walls, the floor, or the ceiling, but his movements are disproportionate, are nervously indecisive. At the end of two hours, he (Jacinto) believes that his task is finished, and sits down again on the corner of the cot. Suddenly he notices a sensation of heat and itching, unbuttons his shirt and scratches himself vigorously. He notices something strange, unbuttons another button, bends his head and looks. Jacinto was never a man with hair on his chest, and yet now, over his breastbone, thick fleece is sprouting, beige-colored, which simultaneously keeps him warm and gives him an itchy feeling. The color of the fleece doesn't surprise him (Jacinto) because Jacinto is extremely blond, almost an albino, but he is puzzled by this sudden hairy outcropping, for because of his age (forty-four) it's more likely that he would be starting to lose the light fuzz on his calves. He lifts one leg, pushes up his pants, pulls down his sock and examines it (his calf) and Jacinto is perplexed because his shinbones are thin and straight up and down (without a bulge in them), hardly more than a bone covered with hairy white skin. He (Jacinto) lifts the other calf and sees that its shape and appearance are identical to the other one. "It's been a week since I've eaten really well; maybe more," he tells himself. And suddenly, he hears the motor, rrr-rrr-rrrm, an intermittent hum, imperceptibly increasing in volume, which opens an unexpected gash in the lethal silence (except for the crepitation of the stems) that enfolds him. Jacinto jumps to his feet. "A plane!" he shouts to himself. He (Jacinto) stands there motionless, on his feet, his legs apart, slightly flexed, his whole body tense, his head on one side, expectant, until his (Jacinto's) ears catch the sound wave again, rrr-rrr-rrrm, and then he gives another jump and shouts "A plane!" and runs toward the door, but the door doesn't open, it seems to be nailed shut, screwed shut, and meanwhile, the buzz of the motor becomes more and more perceptible and clear, it's getting closer, and Jacinto concentrates his energies in his right shoulder and hurls himself against the door, but the door doesn't budge and Jacinto hurts his shoulder, he mutters, rails at it, plants his feet on the floor, arches his body like a flying buttress and presses on the door with his hands, putting heart and soul into the effort, but the door stays absolutely unchanged, it doesn't move so much as a millimeter, while the hum of the motor increases in volume, grows until it deafens him (Jacinto), swooshes a few meters above the roof, rrrrrrrrm, the windowpanes and the slate shingles vibrate noisily, brrrrrr, and then, it decreases, becomes sharper, is diluted until it almost disappears in the distance. After a few seconds of paralysis, Jacinto takes four giant steps to stand at the kitchen window, raises the glass, climbs on the kitchen bench and pushes out the shutters. The plant growth holds them (the shutters) fast, but a slight back-and-forth movement is possible, they are not held completely fast, and as Jacinto hears again, though very far

193

away, the stuttering of the motor, he becomes impatient, pushes uselessly with his hands and knees, turns around and gives a few shoves with his buttocks, loses his balance and falls, bouncing once, from the bench to the floor (on his feet), again climbs on the bench and, finally, some branches break and a slit opens which, though it is not wide enough to admit his (Jacinto's) body, offers him an overwhelming vegetal panorama: the edges of the hedge have reached heights of four meters and the growth completely covers the well, the shed for the motor, and the tool shack. Jacinto keeps pushing at the shutters and, in view of their (the shutters') resistance, gets desperate and says quite a number of times, "Shit, shit, shit," and with every "Shit, shit, shit," the shutters give way by a few millimeters, but when the airplane, buzzing and whistling, skims over the roof for the second time, rrrrrrm, just a few meters above it, Jacinto loses heart. "It's not going to come back," he says and climbs down from the bench and, with the axe, hacks apart the bed where he sleeps and seizes one of the long sides, puts one end of it between the two shutters and, with all his heart and soul, uses the other end as a lever. The hedge is flattened, the right-hand shutter splinters, and Jacinto shouts for joy. The tangled growth makes his movements difficult but, at the same time, the thick branches and the forks in the plants aid his climb to the eaves, and, once there, he clutches them, bends at the waist and clambers to the roof, also invaded by the stems, leaf buds and runners, which allow him to run along it (the roof) without fear of sliding off. The sunlight blinds him (Jacinto) at first, a strange sensation comes over him, as if he were

194

a fetus brought to birth after forty-four years inside his mother; he closes his eyes and waits. The humming of the motor, rrrrrm, is getting farther away and he (Jacinto) opens his eyes and, though the tips of the hedge are higher than the cabin, he sees, from the angle of the roof, the grove of oak trees (most of them with new leaves), the boulders with their blackish-yellow hollows, the rectangle of reddish plowed earth, and the upper row of hives in the beehive colony. The patch of hedge spreads diabolically around the cabin like a virgin forest. The sun is directly overhead and Jacinto shades his eyes with his hand to see the horizon where he hears (or thinks he hears), very far off, the buzzing of the motor, rrrrrm, rrrrrm, he strains his eyes, squinting through his eyelids and, under a little cumulus cloud, spies a small black spot that emits glints of light and, unable to contain himself, with the same earnestness as if he were speaking to someone more distressed than himself, he cries, "There it is!" and jumps up and down on the slates like a child. But he immediately feels a fear that the airplane will not return, that it has flown over the cabin without seeing it and there is even the possibility (thinks Jacinto) that if it returns, the pilot will not be able to see him (Jacinto) among the dense growth. With the automatic gift for action that he has acquired in recent days, Jacinto does not hesitate, he straddles the roofline and climbs down, feeling with his feet for the forks and knots that will bear his weight, enters the hut, ties a sheet around his waist and returns to the roof by the same route. The buzzing of the plane, rrrm, rrrm, rrrm, is very perceptible now, it comes in concentric waves, alternately sharp and soft, producing a slight vibratory disturbance. Jacinto sees it, very far away, to the left of the cumulus cloud, like a swooping mosquito. It appears to be a two-passenger sport model plane, and something in the cockpit reflects the rays of the sun in an intermittent winking like the twinkling of a heliograph. He (Jacinto) holds the sheet by two of its corners and waves it (the sheet), flaps it up and down nervously, while his (Jacinto's) weakened eyes become wet with tears.

Now the little plane is flying high, not intending (apparently) to change direction, monotonously, and though the concentric waves of its buzzing surround Jacinto very closely, he (Jacinto) gets frightened and waves the sheet faster and faster, as he shouts, "Here; here I am!" but the plane continues to fly imperturbably in the same direction over the head of the ravine, toward the north, and when it is scarcely more than the size of a gnat, it turns abruptly to the left and dives steeply and Jacinto flaps the sheet like a man possessed and yells, "Here, here, here I am!" and the plane turns toward him and descends even lower, it gradually increases in size and now it is its propeller that sparkles, but Jacinto no longer sees anything (his tears get in the way), and as he hears the deafening rrrrrrrmmm! over his head, he bursts out sobbing and continues to wave the sheet automatically and tells himself, "They've found me; I'm saved," he (Jacinto) says to himself, and he wipes his eyes and sees that the airplane is flying away again and, although he is sure that it (the plane) has flown over the cabin at a height of less than twenty meters, uncertainty begins to gnaw at him, he climbs on the chimney and stands up there (in this position he can see all three rows of bee-hives, and the ruins of the mill with the two abandoned millstones, and the broad field of grama grass, like an oasis, in the oak grove), the sheet in his hands, and he waves it (the sheet) up and down again, and, again, the airplane veers to port, dives steeply, roars, turns toward him (Jacinto), gets dizzyingly close, grows by the second (like a huge inflated dragonfly) aiming straight at his head, with a thunderous noise, rrrra-rrrra-rrrraaa, in a suicidal pass so close that Jacinto lets go of the sheet and barely has time to fling himself face down on the roof to escape being decapitated. It hurts his ribs considerably, but Jacinto smiles and says to himself, "Gosh, he almost got me," but he smiles, and seated as he is (his emotion is so strong that his legs won't hold him up) he takes his handkerchief out of his pocket and waves it.

The airplane makes four more passes, skimming the roofline, so low that every time he sees it coming, Jacinto flings himself full length against the roof, seeking the protection of the chimney. In the first (of the last four passes), Jacinto sees the two heads of the crewmen in the cockpit and, during the third pass, despite the goggles and leather helmet, identifies Darío Esteban as the crewman in the back seat, and as the airplane flies over him (over Jacinto) in the last and definitive pass, he does not move a finger, and, however, Darío Esteban smiles at him, focusing his binoculars on him; he lifts his right hand with the great pastoral ring and waves goodbye, while Jacinto, who has completely collapsed, kneels on the slate shingles, makes a megaphone (around his mouth) with his two hands and shouts with all the force of his lungs:

"Please, Darío Esteban, open up!"

Then he (Jacinto) feels sorrowful and empty. He watches the airplane dwindle in the distance, leaves the sheet and handkerchief on the roof and slides down from the eaves to the window, closes it (only the glass, because one of the shutters is ruined, and the other is immobilized by tendrils) and although he doesn't say anything he thinks, "All is lost," that is what he (Jacinto) thinks, and in front of the mirror in the toilet (gentlemen) he asks himself stupidly if this business (his situation) is a homicide, a suicide, or a vegetable murder (his imagination, in the last resort, breaks out into a feverish delirium). "Don Abdón gave me the seed, Darío Esteban ordered me to plant it, and I watered it; now the hedge is strangling me. No judge will be able to fix responsibilities," he tells himself. He twists his medal around and around while he tries to find, intuitively, among vague, misty ideas, a juridico-penal figure to fit his case. It is his last consolation. He (Jacinto) steps closer and closer to the mirror and sees close up his stupefied eyes (all pupils), his slanting, stubborn-looking forehead, his ears like fans (covered with down), his nose prominent, blackened at the tip, almost joining the blank, absurdly smiling line of the mouth that gapes below. Unexpectedly he aims a blow with his fist at the glass, which breaks into a thousand pieces:

"They've suicided you, jacinto!" he yells.

Suddenly he (jacinto) is invaded by a peaceful, restful feeling, a gentle sense of acceptance. As he returns to the bedroom he sees the vegetal stalactites and stalagmites, the stiff leaves, the limp yellow flowers of the hedge, but they no longer cause him anguish; jacinto has done away with past and future and sees only the immediate present, and the immediate present does not displease him: it is neither hot nor cold in the hut, it does not smell bad, there are a comfortable mattress and sufficient provisions. However, jacinto feels an invincible desire to curl up, to lie down on the floor and he thinks fleetingly (and with absolute calmness) that perhaps this is the call of the earth. Finally, he squats, places his hands and knees on the floor tiles and moves forward with amazing agility. And he enjoys walking like this, on all fours, and looks greedily at the tempting green leaves that hang from the ceiling or push in through the cracks in the walls and the joints of the window frames. He (jacinto) approaches the lowest of them (the leaves), opens his mouth, clips them off with his herbivorous incisor teeth, and gobbles them down in a trice. Their consistency (that of the leaves) is a bit harsh, but as he chews them they exude a slightly bitter juice which jacinto finds pleasant and stimulating. Again he bites and eats, unhurriedly, and then, he repeats this again and again until not a single leaf is left in the living room and jacinto falls over sideways, but the blue sweater chafes under his arms and the black pants are tight in the groin and, in view of this, and in view of the fact that he is alone, and in view of the fact that no one can come and scold him, he takes them off (sweater and pants) and also takes off his shirt, undershirt, shorts, socks, and shoes and is naked with nothing on but the medal around his neck. He (jacinto) observes, somewhat surprised but not perplexed, the dense tufts that hang from his chest and belly and even the upper part of his thighs. He also looks at his private parts, which are well preserved and very much diminished in size. But he sees all this from the outside, as if he were another person; he does not analyze it, it does not interest him (jacinto). He feels an itch in his belly and, contrary to his usual habits, scratches himself insistently with his foot, scritch-scritch-scratch, whose size (the foot's) is ridiculously small but strong and tough. After that, he raises his head and sees the branch hanging over the mattress, temptingly loaded with leaves and, on all fours as he is, he jumps up on the mattress and in a few seconds has stripped it (the branch) of its leaves, with small but calculated bites. When he finishes, jacinto, deliberately, instead of climbing down from the mattress in a human fashion, first placing one foot on the floor and then the other, throws himself off sideways like a ball, but the fleece covering his body is so thick that it seems to jacinto that the floor tiles have springs in them, they bounce (him) and then, he (jacinto) returns to the mattress and repeats the fall and laughs, or rather gurgles, and the game amuses him so much that for an hour he does nothing but roll off onto the tiles just to enjoy the pleasant pillowy sensation of the impacts. When an hour has passed, jacinto feels tired and lies down. But, strangely, he (jacinto) doesn't use the mattress to do this, as was traditional for him, but settles down in the darkest corner of the cabin, next to the door (after scratching himself against it), and he does not lie on his left side, with his feet drawn up and his hands at his breast as he has done since he was a child, but lies face down, his arms stretched out in front of him and his legs drawn up under his belly. And although the crackling noises, crick-crick, and the impacts, pop-pop, of the ceiling boards and loosened chunks of plaster are more and more frequent, jacinto does not budge, he nibbles lackadaisically at the tender shoots that are pushing up between the floor tiles near him, or amuses himself by watching the gold medal around his neck swing to and fro. But no matter what he does, he (Jacinto) likes having his head low, humbled, a posture which gives him a very special perspective, not precisely an aerial perspective but quite the opposite, a perspective from below looking upward, a lowly perspective to give it a concrete name, so that all of the few things around him (jacinto), bed, fireplace, lamps, metal skeleton of the bookcase, windows, etc., everything, strikes him as higher and more conspicuous than he is.

At intervals, he gets up and lies down again (suddenly, the better to enjoy his padded falls), always in the darkest corners and, occasionally, he drops off, lies in a sort of trance, and then he is assailed by very rapid and varied dreams, often unpleasant, as when he dreams that Gen is running after him asking for water, wa-wa-wa-, loudly, and biting him on the bottom and at other times extremely pleasant, as when he seems to be lost in the immense fields of sugar beets and alfalfa that surround the city, and no one is there to keep him from eating all he wants. No sooner does he awake from one of these dreams (particularly the pleasant ones), than jacinto feels hungry and as the stems that are sticking through the cracks in the cabin are tasty and tender, he (jacinto) can sate it (his hunger) without having to move from the spot.

201

And as soon as he has finished eating, he goes to sleep again; and as soon as he has finished sleeping (having a little nap), he (jacinto) eats again. And if between eating and sleeping he feels an urgent need, jacinto doesn't bother to go to the toilet (gentlemen), he simply compresses the muscles of his belly right there where he is and the goatish droppings roll along the floor noiselessly and with no bad smell.

Meanwhile, the hedge's pressure has made the shutters in the living room explode. The explosion has been short and violent, booooooom! like a cannon shot, to the point that it awakens jacinto who had been sleeping with his head tucked into the fleece on his chest, but he (jacinto) merely raises his head (whose forehead is becoming more slanted and narrow by the moment), observes with vague eyes the window where the hedge has burst in and, immediately, hides his head again among the woolly tufts on his breast as if nothing that happens anywhere around him affects him (jacinto) directly. Thus a moment comes when the leaves, tendrils, shoots, and flowers of the hedge (less intense in color than those that grow outside) surround jacinto and he (jacinto) does not need to stand up and eat, and so he eats and sleeps, sleeps and eats (which is the only thing he cares about doing for the moment) without changing his position, simply moving his head from one side to the other, but then a difficulty arises; when after several hours jacinto tries to stand up to stretch his legs, he observes with indifferent surprise that his two ankles are fastened together by a creeper and when he notices this his indifference is so great that, instead of lopping off the stems that are holding him fast in order to free his feet, he lies down quietly again and closes his eyes.

A sharp stab galvanizes him (jacinto), makes him turn over, though with no desire for retaliation, and he tries to stand up, but the grave, conciliatory voice of Darío Esteban, beside him, reassures him:

"Be quiet, jacintosanjosé, it's only a moment," he says, placing the hand with the ring on it upon his fleece. "Everything will be fine, don't worry."

Jacinto opens his eyes. He (jacinto) is lying on a chromeplated folding table, on the right side of the table are the two doctors (the one who acquired Gen's head and his younger colleague) and, on the other side of the table, Darío Esteban. Some distance away, on the hillside, Serafín is strolling in the sun with a cigarette in his hand between the cherry-colored car and the red-painted hedge-cutting machine, with a foreign name under the motor. On another, smaller table, also chromeplated, the doctors have improvised an emergency medical kit: silver-colored instruments, rolls of cotton, gauze, flasks, syringes, and a large pile of medicines. Jacinto, docilely, lets them do whatever they like. Now the older doctor searches for his heart under his fleece, while the younger one makes him open his right eye. Then they look in his mouth, holding down his tongue with a wooden tongue depressor, fasten a rubber gadget around his arm and repeatedly flex both legs, which are jointed in the opposite direction from the normal one. Darío Esteban, who is observing the examination with professional eyes, softly repeats, "Be quiet, jacintosanjosé, don't move. It's a routine examination; they'll finish right away. Fortunately we've arrived in time. Who could imagine this capacity for growth in the American hybrid?"

Jacinto tries to answer, but notices a sensation as if someone has forced two removable bridges into his mouth, one upstairs and one downstairs, so that neither the shape of his tongue nor that of his palate are capable of pronouncing words, and in view of this, he stops trying. Now the doctors are opening his legs and touching his private parts, but jacinto does not feel the slightest shame, he submits to everything and the older doctor turns to Darío Esteban with an admiring grin and says, "By gum! He's a splendid stud for breeding-ewes," he says. Then he gives jacinto a friendly pat on his rump and adds, "Off with you!"

Jacinto jumps off the table to the floor on all fours, runs unsurprisedly through the broad open space which divides the hedge like a firebreak and emerges into the light. The cherry-colored car is parked on the road, and a little farther off, among the thyme and groundberry plants, the red-painted hedge-cutting machine with the foreign name under the motor. Beside it, Serafín smoking. Jacinto crosses the road near him (near Serafín) without greeting him. Jacinto has already forgotten the medical examination. He only notices the sun overhead, the mountain breeze, the perfume of thyme and rosemary, a pleasant sensation as he steps on the carpets of groundberry, the chirping of the birds, teet-cheep-piu-piu, and the murmur of the brook as it brushes past the willows, slap-slap, the objects around him (ruined mill, beehives, underbrush, oak trees) without meaning. But none of those things makes any impression on him, arouses a desire in him, or stimulates him. He is simply imbued with the idea that he is alive; that he is. Suddenly he spies on the opposite hillside the oasis of grama grass and, without thinking, starts to run down the slope. As he runs he hears a tinkling noise nearby, tinkle-tinkle-tinkle, and stops to verify where it comes from, in view of his suspicion that he is being followed, and when he finds out that he is not (being followed), he continues to frisk along, more impatient by the moment, and, as he runs, he realizes that what is hanging around his neck is not a medal but a sheep-bell, and that it is not a chain which holds it (the bell) in place but a stiff leather collar, and at each jump, among the tussocks and pebbles, the musical tinkling (of the bell), tinkle-tinkle-tinkle, sounds forth, and this musical accompaniment encourages and calms him, and jacinto feels happy because he knows how to produce that sound, and stimulated by it (and by the oasis of grama grass) he hops agilely over the waters of the brook (producing momentum with his legs and clinging to the opposite bank with his hands, which have become much smaller and harder, like two calloused stumps) and now he notices as he clambers up the slope, among oak thickets, thornbushes, and crags, that he is not getting tired, nor slipping, nor do his naked limbs hurt him, but that this is his proper environment, and as he reaches the island of grama grass he stops, lowers his head to the ground, but suddenly remembers Darío Esteban and although he is drooling (for saliva is running into his mouth), he desists, climbs to the top of a nearby boulder and from its summit sees him (Darío Esteban) on the opposite side, standing with the doctors next to the cherry-colored car, in front of Serafín and the red hedge-cutting machine, and wants to yell to him, "Hey! Here I am, Darío Esteban, don't worry, I'm coming right down!" he wants to yell to him, and he tries to adapt his tongue to this effort and he (Jacinto) opens his mouth, but he only cries, "Baaaaaaaaa!"

And the ravine instantly replies, "Baaaaaaaaa!"